SPRING OR CRUEL WINTER?
THE EVOLUTION OF THE ARAB REVOLUTIONS

Dr. Alon Ben-Meir

Westphalia Press
An imprint of the Policy Studies Organization

Washington, DC
2014

Spring or Cruel Winter:
The Evolution of the Arab Revolutions
All Rights Reserved © 2014 by Policy Studies Organization

Westphalia Press
An imprint of Policy Studies Organization
1527 New Hampshire Ave., NW
Washington, D.C. 20036
info@ipsonet.org

ISBN-13: 978-1-941472-93-4

Cover design by Taillefer Long at Illuminated Stories:
www.illuminatedstories.com

Daniel Gutierrez-Sandoval, Executive Director
PSO and Westphalia Press

Devin Proctor, Director of Media and Publications
PSO and Westphalia Press

Updated material and comments on this edition
can be found at the Westphalia Press website:
www.westphaliapress.org

CONTENTS

SPRING OR CRUEL WINTER?
THE EVOLUTION OF THE ARAB REVOLUTIONS

OVERVIEW

OVERVIEW

Overview of the Arab Spring

November 3, 2011

The term "Arab Spring" was coined to suggest the advent of a new era of awakening that would engulf the Arab world and serve as a harbinger of a new socioeconomic and political order. A few lessons can be learned from what has already emerged since the first uprising was sparked in Tunisia in December of 2010. However, the only certainty that can be deduced from the uprisings that have occurred throughout the Middle East and North Africa is that the Arab world will never be the same again.

This essay proceeds in ten sections. The first two sections analyze the Arab uprising as an integral part of global transformation, ushering in a new era in which no ruler can deprive his citizens of their basic rights. The next four sections explain how common denominators and unique characteristics of each country, as well as determinants of Western intervention, will shape the development of each nation's respective uprising and future. This part will demonstrate why the Arab "Spring" could turn into a cruel "winter" of new challenges and political uncertainty. Many of these difficulties will stem from weak foundations of political and economic development. Such an environment will present conditions that are conducive to an Islamist takeover, and whether or not that does occur, Islamic principles will certainly be incorporated into each country in various degrees as the emerging political order takes shape.

The following sections discuss the regional implications of the Arab Spring: both its potential expansion into the Gulf countries and the openings it offers for regional powers to exploit the uncertainties to their advantage. The article concludes by suggesting that political reforms must be accompanied by economic development programs to guide the transitions and avoid violent protests in the Arab countries that have been spared upheavals.

1. THE ARAB UPRISING SUGGESTS THE ADVENT OF A NEW ERA

Some scholars, such as George Friedman, have suggested fallacious notions about the 'Arab Spring': that it is a kind of mass delusion that amounts to no more than "some demonstrations accompanied by slaughter and extraordinarily vacuous observers."[1] When university graduate turned street vendor Mohamed Bouazizi set himself on fire in front of a government building in Sid Bouzid, Tunisia, he unleashed a torrent of long repressed political expression in the Middle East. Through his brave self-immolation, he sent a clear message to his generation: die with dignity rather than continue to live and suffer the daily indignities that amount to an unfulfilled life. It is that message that incited Egyptians, Yemenis, Libyans, Syrians and others to protest and die in the hope that their sacrifices would bring an end to the daily injustices they had to endure.

The ethos of protest began growing in the Arab world several years ago. In their 2007 *National Interest* article entitled "Arab Spring Fever," Nathan J. Brown and Amr Hamzawy aptly observed that the unusual protests in the streets of the Middle East from 2005-2007 indicated that "dreams of democratic openings, competitive elections, the rule of law and wider political freedoms have captured the imagination of clear majorities in the Arab world."[2]

Those who never expected the Arab youth to rise against their authoritarian governments were proven wrong. The Arab youth of today are not the same youth of a generation ago. This new generation has been exposed to the world at large. They have risen against oppression, deprivation, and stagnation, and they no longer want to live under corrupt leaders and governments. An assumption that the Arab youth will indefinitely remain subject to the whims of despots would be an insult to a people who have contributed so much to civilization and enlightenment. No Arab government, however oppressive, will ever be in a position to completely cut off access to the outside world or stifle the desire for freedom from its youth. The revolutionary mindset of the youth may fluctuate in intensity, but it is not a passing phenomenon. It will last for many years and wind down only when new or current Arab regimes commit to, and deliver on, promises for constructive reforms.

The 2011 uprisings were neither instigated by outside powers or criminal gangs, as some Arab leaders have suggested, nor did the revolutionaries need to blame outside entities for their problems. The demonstrators did not even ask for foreign interventions

---

1 George Friedman, "Obama and the Arab Spring," *Townhall.com*, May 26, 2011. Available at: http://finance.townhall.com/columnists/georgefriedman/2011/05/26/obama_and_the_arab_spring/page/full/
2 Nathan J. Brown and Amr Hamzawy, "Arab Spring Fever," *National Interest* (September/October 2007): 33-40.

unless faced with a regime willing to massacre its people to remain in power, such as Qaddafi's Libya. These youth did not blame Israel or the United States for their country's failures, and instead pointed the finger at their own leaders.

Typically, the regimes of Mubarak, Assad, Qaddafi, and Saleh have attempted to portray the uprising as a foreign-instigated conspiracy.[3] This has been done in vain, as the revolutionary-minded youth refuse to be swayed by the empty slogans and contrived excuses of those in power, who suggest that chaos will dominate in their absence. Gone are the days when Arab leaders could ride the wave of public discontent by blaming Israel, the United States, or former colonial powers for their trying existence. For a long time, the Arab youth has been following stories of Israel bringing its top leaders to justice for corruption. They then compare these stories with the situations in their own countries where corrupt leaders have been in power for decades.

2. THE ARAB SPRING IS AN INTEGRAL PART OF GLOBAL TRANSFORMATION

The Arab uprising must be seen as an integral part of a world in transformation. Technological and informational revolutions have increased globalization and interconnectedness between cultures. This linkage makes it impossible for tyrants to rule for the entirety of their lifetimes while mercilessly subjugating their peoples to lives of servitude, with no prospect of ever experiencing freedom. The uprisings of the present have been organized via online social networking sites such as Facebook and Twitter, enabling the movements to become televised, texted, and tweeted. The *Al-Jazeera* Arabic news network has marginalized state media coverage and delivers messages to the ordinary, less "socially networked" masses. These networking and media outlets, of course, did not make political revolutions happen. Rather, they have been on the frontline of the revolutions, precluding the need for ideological leadership to direct them. Attempts by the regimes to cut off their populations from the rest of the world by shutting down telephone and internet services proved counterproductive: it both highlighted that rulers were attempting to cover up their people's outrage, and widely confirmed their lack of responsibility towards their own people.

New media has enabled revolutions to spread domestically, as well as beyond national borders. Arab regimes failed miserably to oppress the Arab Spring because, as F. Gregory Gause has argued, this "very leaderless quality of the popular mobilization" is what "made

---

3 Christiane Amanpour, "Suleiman: Egypt will not be anything like Tunisia," *ABC News*, February 3, 2011; see also Abdel-Haleem Salem, "Alleged agreement between Israel and Libya rebels," *Alyoum Alsabea*, May 15, 2011.

them sources of inspiration."[4] But it has also rendered the mobilization virtually impervious to the security apparatus. This is why the protest that started over rampant unemployment and corruption in Tunisia led to the ouster of Tunisian President Zine El-Abidine Ben Ali and inspired protests in many other Arab countries for their leaders to follow him.

Contrary to what some commentators have said, the Arab uprisings are *not* a divorced phenomenon from the protests that have taken over many parts of the Western world due to the continuing economic crisis. Despite the unique characteristics of each country's situation, the common theme of the protests in the Arab world and the West has been shaped by the continuing world economic crisis, expanding economic inequality, and rising social injustices. Massive budget cuts and raised taxes have led to violent protests in Britain, Spain, Italy, Greece, and elsewhere in Europe. In Israel the gulf between the very rich and the very poor is widening, and skyrocketing living costs have provoked protests. Also, there is a growing belief that a handful of strong private sector groups are dictating the country's economic and social programs, rather than the people's elected representatives.[5] The "Occupy Wall Street" movement sees the root cause of the social and economic inequality in corporate greed and government mismanagement of its power and influence. Arabs, Europeans, Israelis, and Americans have all pointed their fingers at those they believe to be responsible for their problems.

For these protestors democracy is preferred, but they feel that the system does not function well due to exploitation by those with influence. This is why these protesters are seeking reforms and even more drastic measures, including a complete overhaul of the current system. Conversely, the Arab youth see the root cause of their problems to be the authoritarian governments that created and sustained their miserable conditions. They have not experienced freedom and democracy and see no prospect of meaningful change from the current regimes and that is why they are seeking an "overthrow" of the system.

3. THE ARAB SPRING USHERS IN A LONG AND CRUEL WINTER

The Arab Spring will sadly turn into a long and cruel winter, beset with new uncertainties. There are many elements that will make transformation in the Arab world slow, bloody, and full of obstacles. Among these are the lack of traditional liberalism; the consolidation of power within tribes, ethnic minorities, or the military; control of business by the elites; and religious division and extremism.

---

4 F. Gregory Gause III, "Why Middle East Studies Missed the Arab Spring," *Foreign Affairs* 90, no. 4 (July/August 2011), 88.

5 Nahum Barnea, "Say no to American Way," *Yediot Ahronoth*, March 10, 2011.

In Bahrain, the apparent quiet in the country following the Saudi intervention is misleading. The demands of its predominantly Shiite Muslim population for their fair share of political power and economic opportunity, against the discrimination practiced by the Sunni ruling royal family, are not likely to fade away. The tiny island does not have sufficient financial resources to fund Saudi and Kuwaiti-like handouts to placate its citizens. Meanwhile, the show trials of Shiite protesters, with many being sentenced to several years or life prison terms, are likely to feed greater resentment toward the state.[6]

In Syria, the brutal crackdown has created so much hatred that, even if the protests are crushed, it is only a matter of time before they are resurrected. At the same time, the prospect of a sectarian conflict is looming large. Syria's Alawite ruling minority and the Sunni majority are becoming mortal enemies. Random killings against civilians are committed not only by the government forces, but also by members of the Alawite community.[7] The influence of Maher Assad (Bashar's brother) and the Alawite elite leading the regime's unyielding policy prevents any attempt to reverse direction.[8] The protesters are no longer peaceful and people on both sides in Syria are buying weapons smuggled in from Lebanon, not only for self-defense but also to carry out offensive attacks.[9] More troubling for the regime is the growing number of Syria's military rank-and-file who are now defecting for refusing to shoot their fellow citizens.[10] Not only is defection contagious, threatening the coherence of the Assad regime, but also these combat-trained soldiers have already formed an organized armed opposition – the Free Syrian Army – aiming at liberating Syria from Assad's government.[11] Uncontained, such a situation could turn into another post-Saddam Iraq, where vendetta prevails between Sunni and Shiites rather than the rule of law.

Even in those countries where the 'Arab Spring' has already toppled the regime, the real challenges for a new government are just beginning. In Tunisia, the elections of October have marked a milestone in the road to writing a new constitution. However, the victory of Ennahda, the Islamic party, stands to challenge the secular foundation of Tunisia. Conflict between the religious and the secular forces could turn into violence, as seen recently with the attack on the secular *Nessma* TV channel premises in Tunis by Salafist groups protesting against broadcast content.[12]

---

6 Robert Joyce, "Sham trials in Bahrain prove need for greater U.S. pressure," *Human Rights First*, June 28, 2011.
7 Nicholas Blanford, "Syrian refugees describe gangs fomenting sectarian strife," *Christian Science Monitor*, May 17, 2011.
8 Katherine Zoepf and Anthony Shadid, "Syrian Leader's Brother Seen as Enforcer of Crackdown," *New York Times*, June 7, 2011.
9 Arieh O'sullivan, "Syria's Alawites go on arms shopping spree," *Jerusalem Post*, October 16, 2011.
10 Louis Charbonneau, "Syrian soldiers defecting in increasing numbers: U.N.," *Reuters*, November 9, 2011.
11 Tha'ir Abbas, "Asharq Al-Awsat visits the Free Syrian Army," *Asharq Al-Awsat*, October 9, 2011.
12 "Tunisian Salafists attacks TV station for screening film on Iran revolution," *Alarabiya.net*, October 9, 2011. Available at: http://www.alarabiya.net/articles/2011/10/09/170965.html

In Egypt, a failed state could eventually emerge. Many Egyptians would agree that their country is already in a state of chaos with the collapse of the police force, an unprecedented rise in the crime rate, the endless strikes by professionals, and the uncertain "road map" for a transition of power from the military to a civilian government.[13] Additionally, the sectarian violence between Muslims and Christian Copts may threaten the unity of one of the oldest civilizations on earth.

In post-Qaddafi Libya, the process of rebuilding the state will be long, difficult, and punctuated by violence. The situation might not be settled for years to come, and it has a high probability of turning into chaos or civil war as a growing number of rebels refuse to surrender their arms.[14] Ongoing clashes within the rebel groups themselves and between the pro-Qaddafi tribes and those who fought against them with the help of NATO forces could potentially last for the foreseeable future.[15] Those in the United States and the European Union who think that they can get cheap oil and prevent the flow of refugees from Libyan shores might be proven wrong. The oil fields could become an easy target for insurgents, especially if they receive support from Qaddafi's surviving loyalists, who have committed themselves to resistance and avenging his killing.[16]

4. THE INTERNAL CONDITIONS DETERMINE BOTH PROCESS AND OUTCOME

Internal conditions in each of the Arab countries have significantly impacted the development of their respective uprisings, and the same unique conditions will influence each country's post-dictator environment. Each nation in the region also has its own specific characteristics and individual grievances that will shape its future, including: history and culture; demographic composition; the role of the military; resources; geo-strategic situation; and the "legacy of its leader."

Egypt has a largely homogenous population with a Sunni Muslim majority and a Christian Copt minority. The Copts are not ethnically different from the Sunnis, and their peaceful coexistence has been long cited as a model despite the clashes in the last few years. The military is relatively professional and perceives itself as the guardian of the nation, not the personal instrument of a single ruler. President Mubarak, albeit an authoritarian ruler, led his country by a method of political moderation and secularism.

13 Heba Saleh, "Business struggle with insecurity in Egypt," *Financial Times*, November 2, 2011.
14 J. David Goodman, "Libyan Leader Says Militia Clashes Could Create Civil War," *New York Times*, January 4, 2012.
15 Gabriel Gatehouse, "Libya militias clash in Gharyan near Tripoli," *BBC News*, January 16, 2012.
16 AFP, "Gaddafi loyalists thirst for revenge," *The Daily Star*, November 2, 2011.

Tunisia also has had a secular and nationalist foundation since its independence in 1956. The military in Tunisia is deliberately marginalized from political life, and is relatively professional, keeping strong relationships with Western countries. Ben Ali's presidency has been characterized by oppressing Islamic political parties, pushing for secularism, and significantly investing in education.

Libya, Syria, and Yemen are essentially a collection of tribes living under a single state flag. That is because their populations constitute myriad tribes and sects that came to share national territory thanks to the arbitrary borders drawn by colonial powers. But they have never been a unified citizenry, and the disunity was maintained by military dictators. To remain in power, each dictator has relied on an exclusionary political system that depends upon the support of his own tribe and family members. Syria's Alawite minority is ruling over a Sunni majority who views them unfavorably. In Libya, Qaddafi drew the ruling elite from his own tribe, al-Qaddadfa, and his sons. And in Yemen, Saleh's lieutenants are recruited mainly from his tribe, Hashed, and other northern tribes, excluding the South and the Shiites of the country. Within this framework, the militaries in Libya, Syria, and Yemen have been serving as the personal instrument of the ruler, with elite units led by their immediate family members.

The tribe-led countries featured a similar governmental structure, but there were differences in the ruling style of each leader. In Libya, Qaddafi used the state internal security forces against his own people, and denied them any semblance of participatory governance. He also wasted the county's oil resources on pet projects, and on buying an image of leadership in the Arab world and Africa. In Syria, ruthless crushing of protests is a family tradition. In 1982 Rifaat Assad, Bashar's uncle, quelled a revolt in the city of Hama by killing nearly 20,000 of its residents, and the regime of his brother and Bashar's father, Hafez, survived.[17] Yemen, the Arab world's poorest country, has been in an ongoing civil war ever since the forced unification of 1990, and state weakness allowed the emergence of safe havens for Al Qaeda operatives directing attacks against the United States.

Undoubtedly, the unique characteristics of each country have defined their popular movements. They should also influence their respective transitions, and raise the differences between them and other potential uprisings elsewhere in the Arab world. Strong nationalist and secular foundations in Tunisia have enabled the revolution to be essentially devoid of Islamist—not Islamic—elements. Others in the Arab world may not be so fortunate. In Egypt, the Muslim Brotherhood has largely assumed a more cautious

---

17 Robert Fisk, "Freedom, democracy, and human rights in Syria," *Independent*, September 16, 2010.

approach for fear that their otherwise boisterous stand could lead to quick and violent retributions by the military, which has sided with the protesters.[18]

The Libyan National Transitional Council only succeeded in overthrowing Qaddafi because of the help of NATO in a protracted and bloody conflict. Free of international intervention, the regimes in Syria and Yemen—who seem to be living by the motto "rule or die" — are fighting the protests with force, thereby introducing conditions that could lead to a civil war.

5. ISLAM WILL PLAY SIGNIFICANT ROLE IN ANY NEW CONSTITUTION

Few Muslims would dispute the notion that Islam should guide their private and public lives, since the Quran and the Sunna—the tradition of Prophet Muhammad and the two primary sources of Islam's religious law—provide instructions on virtually every aspect of life. More importantly, whether it is the Muslim Brotherhood in Egypt, Syria, and Jordan, or the Ennadha Party in Tunisia, Islamic groups and organizations constitute the best-organized and most well-financed political forces in the Arab world. The results of the parliamentary elections in Tunisia and Egypt, in which the Islamic parties scored dominant victories, highlight the political power that Islamic parties will have in any post-dictatorship government in these countries.

Islamic parties might provide a more permanent and even predictable course of action. However, it is more difficult to predict the extent to which they might moderate their approach to meet the demands of the protesters. Islamic forces in the Arab world should demonstrate their relevance to everyday concerns; emphasize faith; show a commitment to improving the Muslim community. This is especially true at a time when the people are becoming wary about the interplay between politics and religion, as they have seen dubious results in existing Islamic government systems.

Initial signs of a viable Islamic influence on government have already begun to appear. In revolutionary Egypt, the Islamic group Jamat al-Islamiyya has begun looking for a form of Islamic liberalism that is inclusive of other political forces in society.[19] In Tunisia and Libya, where Islamic parties are expected to form a large part of the post-dictatorship governments, the leaders and citizens tend to reject the Saudi and Taliban models and look instead to the Malaysian and Indonesian governmental models that combine Islam with modernity.[20] If this approach is sincere and given enough effort to

---

18 *The Daily Star*, "Egyptians extend protest but Muslim Brotherhood abstains," July 16, 2011.
19 Emad Mekay, "In Egypt, Islamists Reach Out to Wary Secularists," *New York Times*, September 21, 2011.
20 Anthony Shadid and David D. Kirkpatrick, "Activists in Arab World Vie to Define Islamic State," *New York Times*, September 30, 2011.

mature into coherent policy, it would lead to the emergence of a democratic Islamic state model that would respond to the reforms Muslim societies require.

Islamic parties could in fact be the element in society that bridges the gap between the people and their government, as the majority of their activities have historically been composed of providing social services at the grassroots level.[21] Furthermore, the bottom-up participatory approach to establishing sub-nationally driven development can be illustrated by Islamic concepts. Islamic banking is becoming an increasingly more attractive alternative to Western banking[22] as its interest-free finance—based on Shari'a prohibition of payment for loans of money—responds to the very dilemmas that caused the current global economic crisis. This could lead already-growing Islamic banking to thrive, and offer some examples of how to modify business practices within the rules of Shari'a. Typifying this model is the experience of Bangladesh's Muhammad Yunus whose microfinance project with the Grameen Bank, which provides micro-credit to poor people possessing no collateral, earned him the 2006 Nobel Peace Prize. In sum, regardless of the political order that emerges from the Arab Spring, there will always be an Islamic component incorporated into the new political system.

6. GEOPOLITICS AND RESOURCES DETERMINE OUTSIDE INTERFERENCE

Geostrategic considerations have also influenced the international community's reaction to the uprisings in each country. European Union concerns over oil production and the potential by-products of Qaddafi's brutal response to the uprising – a humanitarian crisis, waves of refugees, as well as potential terrorist activities across the Mediterranean – pushed NATO into intervention in Libya.[23] President Obama's determined approach with Mubarak was primarily motivated by the potential impact a chaotic Egypt could have on relations with Israel and the Palestinians, as well as the vast U.S. investments in the Egyptian military.[24]

In other countries, however, the United States and the West are reluctant to intervene. In Bahrain, the protests went largely ignored out of fears that success of the Shiite majority's demands would pave the way for an Iranian foothold in the Arab peninsula, thus setting a precedent for Shiite minorities in Kuwait and Oman and seriously

---

21 Sameh Naguib, "The Muslim Brotherhood: Contradictions and Transformations," *Cairo Papers in Social Science* 29, no. 2/3 (2009): 155-174.

22 Muhammed Idris, "Islamic Finance – An Emerging Alternative: An Analysis of the Islamic Finance Industry in the Context of the Changing Global Financial Industry," *McNair Scholars Journal*, no. 10 (Spring 2010): 87-116.

23 Lance Selfa, "Libya's revolution, U.S. intervention, and the left," *International Socialist Review*, No. 77 (May-June 2011).

24 Joseph Weber, "Clinton warns against 'chaos' in Egypt," *Washington Times*, January 30, 2011.

endangering U.S.-Saudi relations.[25] Syria holds the key to many issues in the Middle East. The future of the Iran-led "resistance bloc", the country's stock of unconventional weapons, continued stabilization in Iraq, the conflict with Israel, and Turkey's "new eastern policy" all depend on what will happen in Syria. In fact, concern over these issues is what has provided Bashar Assad immunity from international intervention to stop his regime's brutal crackdown of protests.[26] Similar fears over the expansion of Al-Qaeda's network and their possible takeover of the Gulf of Aden in Yemen and Somalia has prevented American intervention against Saleh's regime.[27]

Thus, the perceived strategic importance of each country has seemingly determined the extent of Western interference. However, the double standard in the West could negatively impact President Obama's agenda for democratization and human rights throughout the Middle East. This regional dynamic is made even more complicated by the administration's failure to advance a solution to the Israeli-Palestinian conflict, which is the main cause of resentment of the United States among Arabs.[28] For that reason, what should and can be done is to adjust Western interference in the Arab Spring so that it combines an encouragement of gradual political reforms with economic growth and sustainable development, as explained below.

7. MONARCHIES WILL EXPERIENCE A MORE SETTLED TRANSFORMATION

Generally speaking, the transition in the Arab monarchies will be more peaceful than in other Arab states, but they are likely to experience varying degrees of violence. Arab monarchies understand the socio-economic motivation behind the Arab uprisings in Tunisia, Egypt, Libya, and Yemen. The latest example is in Saudi Arabia, where King Abdullah's $37 billion welfare package for Saudi citizens[29] and a 15 percent raise for government employees sought to stave off any protests against the government before they started.[30] Another is the Bahraini government's one-time payment of $2,650 to each family, in an attempt to buy compliance and silence which has this far been unsuccessful.[31]

25 "Bahrain crackdown ignored by West," *Huffington Post*, September 5, 2011.
26 Michael Silverman, "Syria Isn't Libya: Obama Must Consider Bolder Intervention," *Christian Science Monitor*, December 7, 2011.
27 Osama Al Sharif, "Saleh's dangerous game," *Al-Arabiya News*, October 20, 2011; James M. Dorsey, "Closer ties between Somali and Yemeni Jihadists threatens oil through Aden gulf," Al-Arabiya News, July 18, 2011.
28 Chas W. Freeman, "U.S.-Arab Relations: Forks in the Way Forward," *Middle East Policy* 16, no. 4 (Winter 2009): 68-75.
29 "Saudi Arabia's King Abdullah's $37bn benefits package," *BBC News*, February 24, 2011.
30 Sarah A. Topol, "Saudi King Announces Wage Hikes, Holds Fast Against Political Reform," *AOL News*, February 23, 2011.
31 Rick Jervis, "Cash can be key to quelling dissent," *USA Today*, March 3, 2011.

These are examples of unsustainable, short-term measures that Arab monarchies are taking in an effort to quell public demands for greater freedom and social equality.

The Arab monarchies have yet to recognize other motivations for the protests. They must realize that the public does not want handouts—it wants a voice. The people want to be heard because they recognize their inherent right to be heard, they want to live in dignity and will refuse to settle for their government's reactionary ploys in pursuit of social justice. Oil-rich, Arab Gulf monarchies may avoid uprisings in their home countries by offering these handouts, but they should be well aware that this is only buying time, not stability. As recent field research by Christopher Clary and Mara Karlin has shown, the Saudi population may be satisfied for the moment with the influx of cash, as well as educational and economic diversification that King Abdullah has instituted, but time is critical if he and the royal family wish to avoid a popular revolt.[32]

Regardless of the kind of government Arab states may end up with, adherence to basic human rights and the removal of emergency laws will be central to peaceful transitions. Every Arab King or Emir can gradually pass over some of their powers to a Constitutional Monarchy, where the King or Emir would remain the head of the state, and the prime minister the head of the government with political powers mandated by a popularly elected parliament. A modified version of the British or the Swedish systems of government could be more acceptable both to the royalty as well as to the public. By following this path, current Arab Kings and Emirs can maintain not only the trappings of their positions as heads of state, but can also hold the position of the Commander-in-Chief of the armed forces, allowing them to continue to dictate foreign policy. The Prime Minister, with the backing of an elected parliament, would focus on socio-economic development, education, healthcare, law and order, and the development of the country's infrastructure.

Such a division of power could meet the people's demands and ease the transition of their countries. The change could occur through upheaval and terrifying violence, or it could happen through a peaceful transition.

8. REGIONAL POWERS ARE POISED TO EXPLOIT PROTESTS TO THEIR ADVANTAGE

Each of the regional powers in the Middle East—Egypt, Turkey, Iran, and Saudi Arabia—are poised to exploit the uprising to their advantage. New regional alliances could emerge, or a "cold war" between the competing powers.

32 Christopher Clary and Mara E. Karlin, "Saudi Arabia's Reform Gamble," *Survival: Global Politics and Strategy* 53, no. 5 (October/November 2011): 15-20.

Though poor in resources, Egypt has always been the epicenter of the Arab world. Ideologies originating from Egypt, ranging from Arab nationalism to Islamic fundamentalism, and its political direction, from confrontation with the West and Israel to peaceful relations with them, have dominated the Arab political sphere. Egypt cannot possibly want to risk losing its leadership role in the Arab world. The current Egyptian government has shifted significantly on major foreign policy issues by reaching out to its traditional rivals, Turkey and Iran.[33] But if Egypt is to regain regional leadership, it will inevitably resume its rivalry with these two. Whereas Turkey has initially gained significant popularity in the Arab world, the last thing the Arab governments (and Egypt in particular) want is a return to "Ottoman-style Turkish dominance" or to succumb to Iran's ambition to become a regional hegemon with nuclear weapons capabilities.

Iran wasted no opportunity to describe the Arab uprisings in Tunisia, Egypt, Libya, and Bahrain as an extension of the 1979 Islamic revolution, which it failed to export.[34] The situation is different when it comes to its ally, Syria, which has utilized Iranian weaponry and logistical support to crush its protests. The decision by the Obama administration to withdraw all U.S. forces from Iraq by the end of this year offers Iran an excellent opportunity to expand its support of the Assad regime against the protests. It could also provide opportunity for Iran to extend its influence to create a contiguous Shiite-controlled landmass extending from the Persian Gulf to the Mediterranean Sea. As a result, Syria could feasibly become a battleground between Iran and Turkey, who are determined to shape the outcome of the Syrian upheaval to safeguard their national interest.[35]

Turkey, led by Prime Minister Recep Tayyip Erdogan, has been taken captive by the populist movement. Much like Iran, Erdogan's Turkey aspires to export its "Islamic model" to the Arab Spring countries, exploiting the fact that Islamic forces are likely to dominate future governments.[36] These Islamic groups look favorably on the so-called Turkish model – an economically prosperous democracy living by Islamic values. The danger, however, lies in the disparity between the perception and the reality of the Turkish model in relation to the pervasive power of the Erdogan's AK Party and the sustainability of Turkey's economic prosperity given the global financial crisis, as was demonstrated by the unrest in Taksim Square starting in May 2013. It remains to be seen if Turkey will further intensify its confrontational approach towards Israel or find a way to mend relations, especially since peace between Israel and other Middle Eastern

33 Alon Ben-Meir, "Is this what the revolution is all about?" *Huffington Post*, September 19, 2011.

34 *Haaretz*, "Iran supreme leader: Egypt unrest inspired by our Islamic revolution," February 4, 2011.

35 Alon Ben-Meir, "Keystone Influence: Syria's Arab Spring and the Race for Regional Hegemony," *Huffington Post*, November 28, 2011.

36 Maggie Michael and Lee Keath, "Turkey: Prime Minister Recep Tayyip Erdogan Visits Egypt," *Huffington Post*, September 13, 2011.

countries remains central to regional stability. Historically, those who have opted to divide and conquer or play one country against another, like Nasser's Egypt in the 1960s, risk undermining the very model they once attempted to establish.

9. THE DANGER OF PUSHING FOR QUICK POLITICAL REFORMS

Whereas reforms are needed and necessary, rapid democratic reforms without an orderly and purposeful transitional period combined with economic development programs will fail to produce the desired outcome of a free and vibrant social order. Instead, it could usher in a period of continued instability, or introduce new totalitarian regimes that might assume power under the pretext of maintaining order and stability. No Arab country is ready for comprehensive political reforms without first developing a clear idea of how those reforms should look.

In Egypt, no opposition political party was given an opportunity to organize and campaign freely under the Mubarak regime, which feared that open dissent would pose a real threat to the government's hold on power. There is no culture of political development, and limited experience in country-wide political campaigns, which stifles the growth of civic participation. For this reason, a minimum transitional period of 18-24 months will be needed to allow for the development of secular political parties. A period such as this will enable the parties to establish their political agendas, as well as promulgate their political platforms in a free atmosphere.

The only political party that can quickly surface as a major political force in Egypt is the Muslim Brotherhood, which has quietly but effectively been organizing for many years. The Muslim Brotherhood's Freedom and Justice Party won almost 50 percent of the vote in the parliamentary elections (November 2011–January 2012) and they are now certainly the most powerful political force in Egypt, even without a coalition with the Salafis's Nour party, which received more than 20 percent of the vote.

The same can be said about Libya. In the first post-Qaddafi election (July 2012) and in the writing of the new constitution, political parties had no time to organize, develop political platforms, and familiarize the public with their positions on various issues affecting the country's security and economy. Opting for elections too soon would give much credence and power to isolated tribal factions and Islamists, especially the Libyan Islamic Fighting Group (LIFG), which is the only likely group to be able to garner loyalty in the immature Libyan political landscape.

There are many dangers inherent in quick political reforms. First, any government that would follow a truncated timeframe for elections will most likely lack the broad public support and the required legitimacy to rule, especially after a revolutionary upheaval. In an immature political culture, the challenges to this sort of government would range from endless legal disputes in administrative and constitutional courts, to organized violence by groups who feel they are unjustifiably unrepresented. Second, and more importantly, this government cannot possibly expect to deliver the public's requirements of advances in salaries, services, and economic development – itself the major cause of uprising.

Therefore, an essential part of the transition period in each Arab Spring country will be the implementation of a sustainable economic development campaign driven to immediately help meet critical human needs and introduce and instill democratic practices at the local level. In the Egyptian case, and in many other Arab states, it is important to have this transitional period from authoritarian rule to democracy and a more inclusive market economy to enable a peaceful process to unfold.

10. SUCCESS DEPENDS ON A POWERFUL ECONOMIC DEVELOPMENT PROGRAM

Critical to a peaceful and orderly transition is the immediate undertaking of economic development projects that could begin to provide relief to Arab youth who are despondent and in need of basic commodities. It was deprivation and economic inequality, rather than the desire for political freedom that led to the uprising. That is why revolutionaries and labor in Egypt alike continued demonstrations and strikes. The fall of the regime did not bring what they need: food, jobs, health care and education. There is an inherent relationship between political and economic reforms. In developing, and under-developed countries in particular, the relationship is ever more intertwined; thus, for either to succeed, it is essential to move on both tracks simultaneously.

An essential cause of the Arab uprising is economic underdevelopment. Arab governments tended to favor state-run development projects that cut off economies from international trade and finance. It is no wonder that unemployment rates in these countries have always been in the double-digit area.[37] Generally, when these countries have moved from the socialist economic model to the liberalization and privatization of their economies, the liberalization processes did not lead to sustainable development that could serve as a new source of legitimacy for the regime or enhance its stability. Instead, partly stemming from state corruption and partly from mismanagement, they only have only exacerbated socioeconomic inequality and created a new class of super wealthy entrepreneurs, many of them affiliated with the leaders' families, who have become targets of public discontent.

37 Michael Schuman, "Why the Arab Spring's success depends on jobs, not guns," *Time*, August 22, 2011.

Morocco's post-protest approach, for example, to "wed [democracy and development] together so that each is advanced by way of the other," serves as a good start for reform.[38] Sustainable development occurs through democratic exchanges and consensus-building. Decentralization, which transfers managerial authority, skills, and capacities to sub-national levels, is Morocco's chosen framework to implement democracy and development from the bottom-up.

Considering Morocco's stated goal of decentralization, it follows that its organizational arrangement emphasizes the "participatory method."[39] This democratic approach is to be applied by local communities to assess their development challenges and opportunities, and create and implement action plans that reflect their shared priorities, such as job creation, education, health, and the environment. By extension, the monarchy is apparently open to transformative change of the whole of society, but through a bottom-up process driven by developmentally-empowered and self-reliant local communities.[40] These communities are integrated in a decentralized national system and their elected leaders are chosen based on their ability to help forge and respond to the consensus decisions of their constituents.

Due to the urgency for development projects in countries such as Egypt, Libya, Tunisia and others and the need for their governments' to provide flexibility when responding to the particular socio-economic circumstances of their ever-increasing population, the participatory sustainable development approach is immediately needed.

An integral part of the sustainable development model is the role of Non-Government Organizations (NGOs). NGOs have a greater commitment toward democratic processes and enlisting people's ideas and material contributions for developmental interventions. The goals of local communities organized by NGOs reflect local interest more than government-driven initiatives. The resources NGOs help marshal for development – funded locally or by international donors – include a mix of educational, technical, and material support.

38 Yossef Ben-Meir, "Morocco: Democracy-Building and Sustainable Development," *Morocco Board.com*, March 13, 2011. Available at: http://www.moroccoboard.com/news/34-news-release/5145-morocco-democracy-building-and-sustainable-development.
39 Mohammad el-Ashab, "Strengthening Decentralization in Morocco," *Al-Hayat*, 25 May 25, 2009.
40 Ben-Meir, "Morocco: Democracy-Building and Sustainable Development."

CONCLUSION

The uprising of the Egyptian people following Tunisia's "Jasmine Revolution" has opened a new chapter of change for the Arab world. For the long-entrenched Arab regimes to avoid the same fate as the regimes in Tunisia, Egypt, Libya, and Syria, they must heed the powerful message being expressed on the streets throughout the region. Some Arab tyrants may succeed in subduing popular resistance, but it will take tremendous violence to achieve that. Realizing the inevitability of change, however, a few Arab leaders may now look for an alternative by embracing real reforms. They should do so gradually, systematically, and transparently to convince their publics of their sincerity- Arab governments must listen to their people.

In the transitions, Arab rulers must provide for their people. With the support and encouragement of the West, they should begin by taking five essential steps: 1) institutionalize human rights, 2) build civil society and the culture of political pluralism, 3) provide for economic opportunity and growth, 4) improve education and health care, and 5) crack down on corruption and establish a fair judiciary. Not every Arab state could or should follow the same roadmap for change. But each Arab leader should reassess their political reality and decide on a course of action that would allow them to shape the new order and be hailed as reformers- rather than being forced out of office in disgrace.

Regardless of how ruthless some of these Arab leaders may be, their public will always welcome any improvement in their daily lives. The more consistent and positive these reforms are, the more accepting the people become of an orderly transition. There is such a thing as "benevolent dictatorship" that can rule with mercy, compassion, and understanding, rather than resorting to cruelty, deprivation, and an unruly police state.

EGYPT

EGYPT

EGYPT'S FUTURE RESTS WITH THE MILITARY

FEBRUARY 1, 2011

By now it has become increasingly clear that the future of Egypt's stability, political reforms and progress rest almost entirely in the hands of its military. Unlike militaries in other Arab states, Egypt's is one of the most respected institutions that has earned the admiration and respect of the people. It is, to some extent, similar to the Israeli military. Service in the Egyptian Armed Forces is compulsory, and thus composed of young soldiers from all walks of life with a unique affinity and commitment to the welfare and well-being of their nation.

In that sense it is the people's military, to which most Egyptians look up to with esteem. Although the military supported the Mubarak government, it remained above the fray and largely untainted with corruption, relative to many other government institutions. When a uniformed military spokesman said on state TV that "the armed forces will not resort to use of force against our great people," this strongly suggests that the military not only lived up to the people's expectations, but made the decision not to support the beleaguered President Mubarak if it meant quelling the demonstrators by force. This dramatic turn of events was further reinforced when the same military spokesman, addressing the protesters, said that the military understood "the legitimacy of your demands" and "affirms that freedom of expression through peaceful means is guaranteed to everybody." [1]

One cannot underestimate the critical importance of this development, not only because of its domestic implications but its regional effects, especially in relation to the United States and the peace treaty between Israel and Egypt. Egypt has been and continues to be central to the region's stability. The Mubarak government has worked assiduously to mediate between Israel and the Palestinians and has spared no efforts to limit Hamas' outreach. The belief that without Egypt there will be no new Arab-Israeli

1 Samia Nakhoul, "Egypt army: will not use violence against citizens," *Reuters*, last modified January 31, 2011. http://www.reuters.com/article/2011/01/31/egypt-army-idAFLDE70U2JC20110131.

war and without Syria there will be no comprehensive peace remains valid to this day. Thus, having made the decision in principle not to use force against unarmed Egyptian demonstrators, the military has taken sides and has sent a clear message to President Mubarak that he in fact has two options, albeit neither is very attractive.

The first option is to relinquish power peacefully by establishing a new transitional government completely divorced from current high officials. Under such a scenario, President Mubarak should announce to his nation that he will step down at a specified date no later than September 2011, when new national elections are scheduled. The September date is symbolic for his departure only, although it would be far more prudent to hold the general election after giving the secular opposition parties the opportunity to organize and prepare for a national campaign. For the new transitional government, the President should select respected bureaucrats, which may include Mohamed ElBaradei, former head of the International Atomic Energy Agency (IAEA), around whom most opposition leaders, including those of the Muslim Brotherhood may coalesce. It will then focus for the next 18 to 24 months on preparing the nation for elections while making every effort to revamp the economy, create jobs, address corruption, and undertake political reforms to ensure that the next election will be free and fair. This option will allow Mubarak to leave his office gracefully, something that the Obama administration may well endorse. This will allow for a peaceful transition while offering a much better chance for the secular parties to gain ground compared to the Muslim Brotherhood, which would preserve the peace treaty with Israel - the cornerstone of Middle East stability.

The second option is for Mubarak to resist departing the political scene, in which case the uprising will most likely be further intensified. This scenario bears several unpredictable outcomes, one of which being that it could lead to bloodshed, especially if the internal security forces and police decide to use force against unarmed Egyptians. Extremists like the Muslim Brotherhood may feel more emboldened and try to assert their power, which could end up in major clashes with the military. The prolongation of the unrest will create massive shortages of food, medicine, gasoline and basic necessities, promoting looting, theft and chaos. At the end of the day, if this scenario is to unfold, Mubarak will have to relinquish power and leave his office disgracefully. Many Egyptian scholars and current and former officials with whom I spoke, strongly suggest that the second scenario is not likely to take place because they do not believe that Mubarak would choose this route when in fact he can still leave with some dignity. Others argue that although the Egyptian public is sick and tired of Mubarak's rule, they would like to see their President leave his office with some grace, if for no other reason but to distinguish Egypt from other countries, like Tunisia, where the deposed leader escaped under cover of night.

The stakes for the current reshuffled government remain extremely high. The appointment of General Omar Suleiman, the Director of the Egyptian General Intelligence Directorate, as Egyptian Vice President with a mandate to negotiate with the opposition can take different turns, as General Suleiman himself has a vested interest in preserving the current structure in the hope of inheriting the Presidency. Suleiman's best bet, however, is to work toward the establishment of a transitional government while presenting himself as an honest broker. Knowing him as I do, he is certainly capable of that. The temptation and his strong desire to emerge as the nation's new leader, however, may prevent him from seeing the inevitable. In one way or another the Mubarak regime is finished; the question for General Suleiman will be, does he want to leave like his boss (likely in disgrace under this scenario) or emerge as the healer of the nation and the architect who ushered in a new era in Egypt's history?

Once again, since the 1952 revolution that ended the Egyptian monarchy and brought the military to power, Egypt is facing a historic crossroad. The people, with the support of their military, must now chose the kind of future they seek for Egypt as a country and for its people. They must decide how to utilize what emerges from the ashes of the people's revolution to restore Egypt's leadership as the bulwark of regional stability and peace, and assume the task of promoting freedom, economic progress and growth at home. It is a formidable task, but the Egyptian military, which has shown tremendous capacity for discipline, commitment and love of country, can and may well rise to the occasion.

EGYPT'S DAYS OF GLORY...

...CAN BE SUSTAINED ONLY IF THE REVOLUTIONARIES, THE OPPOSITION FIGURES AND THE ESTABLISHMENT WORK TOGETHER WHILE REALIZING THAT THEY ARE SHAPING EGYPT'S DESTINY

FEBRUARY 9, 2011

I want to begin this column by first applauding the Egyptian people. I applaud them not only for their heroism, but for their tenacity, their deep sense of commitment to their fellow countrymen, the responsibility they have displayed, and their perseverance to see their people's revolution through to its ultimate success. Perhaps none of this is surprising—Egypt, after all, is a country with more than four thousand years of continuing history with unsurpassed cultural riches, a cradle of civilization that has enlightened one generation after another. The revolutionaries stood fast, drawing from their country's glorious history—a history which imbued them with the inner strength and determination to rise again and live up to Egypt's future destiny.

Regardless of how many stages and setbacks this revolution will experience, it cannot and will not fail. It has set in motion a wave of awakening, and neither Egypt nor any of the Arab states will be the same again. Regardless of how the Egyptian revolution ends, its outcome will set the tone for the entire Arab world. No Arab leader will be immune from the revolutionary transformation that will sweep the region, and there is no better time for Egypt to reassume the mantra of leadership as exemplified in the manner in which the revolution is unfolding. The quiet deliberations of a few wise men including the former Egyptian Ambassador to Washington, Nabil Fahmi; the former head of the IAEA, Dr. ElBaradei; Google Executive and compassionate voice of protestors, Wael Ghonim; Muslim Brotherhood Leader, Mohammed Badie; Ghad Party Leader, Ayman Nour; former Member of Parliament and Vice President Omar Suleiman and others, were filled with symbolism and a hard core reality. They were not torn between their loyalty to President Mubarak and the welfare of their people—it was a foregone conclusion that Mubarak must leave. For them, the question was how to orchestrate his departure gracefully, knowing full well that the whole world was watching and that how they conducted themselves would have serious and lasting reverberations throughout the Middle East and beyond.

Although the revolutionaries are tempted, perhaps for good reason, to oust President Mubarak immediately, they must first pause and consider that pushing Mubarak out of power disgracefully will not automatically bring about the reforms they seek. Moreover, his abrupt removal from power will not only humiliate Mubarak himself, but will reflect on Egypt as a country and people who have lost their bearings as they have been engulfed in a revolutionary fervor. Everyone—including President Mubarak—knows that his reign is over. What Egypt needs now is an orderly transfer of power, a transitional period to allow him to finish his term with dignity, albeit with substantially reduced power. The people who have tolerated the Mubarak regime for more than three decades must demonstrate, for Egypt's sake, that regardless of their president's shortcomings, they must act from a historic perspective of Egypt's place and its future role in the Arab world. Mubarak would rather fall on his sword than leave office in disgrace. Those who are negotiating a dignified exit for him must be given every opportunity to finish their task, as long as they remain accountable to the Egyptian people and committed to modernization, economic progress, and political freedom.

Finally, Mubarak's ultimate fate will send a very strong signal to the rest of the Arab states. No Arab leader wants to leave his office in disgrace; they will resist and resort to any coercive means at their disposal to stay in power. Egypt can provide an example of an orderly transfer of power, allowing its leader to depart in a manner befitting Egypt's standing. What the revolutionaries can—and indeed must—do is insist on the immediate repeal of the emergency laws that gave near-unlimited power to the police and other internal security apparatuses that have been known to flagrantly abuse their power. Repealing the emergency laws will give the government some credibility to follow through with other promised reforms.

What is also striking about the Egyptian uprising is the remarkable caring and compassion that most Egyptians displayed toward one another. However chaotic the situation, ordinary Egyptians took care of each other, providing food and medical care where needed. They were not directed by any leaders but assumed responsibility on their own —they chanted together, resisted together, cried with one another, and raised the banner of revolt together. This was a remarkable display of discipline and revealed a capacity to deal with any adverse situation as the uprising evolved. And when they were intimidated and attacked by thugs who appeared to have been dispatched by the Interior Ministry, they fought back together, demonstrating solidarity and an iron-clad will to prevail—and they prevailed. The Interior Ministry realized that this is not a battle they want to win because the consequences of such a "victory" will be far more calamitous.

Also remarkable is the revolutionaries' focus on their own plight. They did not seek a scapegoat to blame for their dismal state of being. They did not blame Israel or the United States for their country's failures and instead pointed the finger at their own leaders. Here again, unlike many other Arabs who blame Israel in particular for all the ills that infect their society, the Egyptians appear to appreciate that their peace with Israel is positive. Whereas Mubarak has failed the Egyptian people by stifling social, economic and political developments, he has managed to ingrain the peace agreement with Israel in the national psyche of the Egyptian people. Even the Muslim Brotherhood vowed to keep the peace treaty with Israel. Indeed, no revolution can make social, political and economic progress by becoming hostile to its neighbors, especially, in this case, Israel—a nuclear power with formidable conventional military capability and with whom Egypt has no quarrel. In fact, Egypt can only benefit from bilateral relations as it has in the past. Moreover, Egyptians understand that each country looks after its own best national interests, including Israel and the US, and it would have been up to the Egyptian authorities to look after the interests of the Egyptian people. It is in that sense that Egypt will again set an example to be emulated by the rest of the Arab states.

Another unique phenomenon is how the Egyptian military behaved throughout the revolutionary process. Being part and parcel of the Egyptian people, the military assumed the responsibility of keeping order in the midst of chaos. They guarded the interests of the nation as a whole and did not follow the government's instinct to subdue the uprising by force. In fact, the opposite was true. The Egyptian military recognized the right of the people to participate in peaceful protest, and refused to take sides while taking security measures it deemed best for the country. The military, to be sure, played an extremely constructive role and must now continue to play such a role by ensuring that there will be a peaceful transitional period while respecting the social and political reforms that the various civilian opposition parties will agree upon. The military will have to continue to act as the guarantor of the state's security, both from within and outside the country. By its own action and behavior, the Egyptian military will send a clear message to other Arab militaries: the military was created to protect the nation mainly from any outside enemy, not to suppress its citizens.

Finally, as the largest, most culturally advanced Arab country, which sets the trend for much of the Arab world, Egypt must now rise to assume its pivotal role in a region riven with instability and competition for regional hegemony, especially between Iran and Turkey. A weak Egypt could leave the Arab world leaderless, creating a vacuum that non-Arab Iran, a predominantly Shiite state, and Turkey, a largely Sunni country, are more than eager to fill. Only Egypt can rise again, not only to lead, but to shield the Arab world from being dominated by a non-Arab state.

The revolution in Egypt has occurred at a most critical time in the Middle East's history. Peace between Israel and the rest of the Arab world remains precarious at best, Iran is racing to acquire nuclear weapons, and Islamic extremist groups are poised to take advantage of failed Arab regimes. The Egyptian revolution offers a clear sign that the old order is finished. The Egyptian people will now shape the new order not only for themselves but for the entire Arab world. The young and brave Egyptian revolutionaries must remember that they—and they alone—will determine Egypt's destiny.

EGYPT'S MESSAGE TO THE ARAB WORLD

FEBRUARY 10, 2011

The uprising of the Egyptian people following Tunisia's "Jasmine Revolution" has awoken the Arab street and signaled a new chapter of change for the Arab world. For the long-entrenched Arab regimes to avoid following the paths of Tunisia and Egypt, they must take heed of the powerful message being expressed on the streets throughout the region. Arab leaders should now learn from Tunisia and especially Egypt's failure by working to address their people's aspirations to enable a stable and gradual transition to greater economic opportunities, better education, human rights, and an end to decades of rampant corruption while guaranteeing political freedoms for their people.

When university graduate-turned street vendor Mohamed Bouazizi set himself on fire in front of a government building in Sid Bouzid, Tunisia, he unleashed a torrent of long-repressed political expression in the Middle East. The subsequent protests against rampant unemployment and corruption in Tunisia and the ousting of Tunisian President Zine El Abidine Ben Ali have led to protests throughout the Arab world, from Algeria to Yemen, with a united refrain to send their leaders to join Ben Ali in his new refuge in Saudi Arabia. The revolt that has subsequently gripped Egypt—the largest and most influential Arab country—has the potential to echo throughout the Middle East. The uprisings have been organized via online social networking sites like Facebook and Twitter, much like the demonstrations against Iran's presidential election last year. It is clear that change is afoot in the region. What is also clear is that for the dictators of the Arab world to manage this change, they must institute genuine social, economic and political reforms immediately while allowing sufficient time for orderly and peaceful transitions.

Some will argue that such reforms, once enacted, will usher an abrupt end to these regimes. I disagree. Regardless of how ruthless some of these Arab leaders may be, their public will always welcome any improvement in their daily lives. And the more consistent and positive these reforms are, the more accepting the people become of an orderly transition while ensuring sustainable growth, developments and social and political reforms. There is such a thing as "benevolent dictatorship" that can rule with mercy, compassion, and understanding without necessarily resorting to cruel methods and deprivations while subjugating everyone to an unruly police state. But in realizing the inevitability of change, many Arab leaders may now look for an alternative by embracing real reforms and doing so gradually, systematically, and transparently to convince the public of their sincerity. To prevent the Tunisian and the Egyptian wave from becoming a tsunami, the

Arab governments of the Middle East must listen to their people. Rapid change from repressive authoritarian regimes to open and transparent democracy, however, is unlikely, and, in fact, not ideal. Islamist extremists are likely to exploit any political vacuum or vulnerability on the difficult path toward democracy. Establishing the culture and infrastructure of democracy—especially where it is a foreign concept—takes time, as we have seen in Iraq, Afghanistan and the Palestinian territories.

However, to provide for their people and take the steam out of the protests, Arab leaders, with the support and encouragement of the West, should begin by taking five essential steps: 1) building civil society and the culture of political pluralism, 2) institutionalizing human rights, 3) providing for economic opportunity and growth, 4) improving education, and 5) cracking down on corruption. Because of its size, centrality in Arab politics, relations with the United States and Israel, and military prowess, what eventually happens in Egypt will reverberate throughout the region and will have a tremendous impact on regional stability and peace. Before any of these critical measures can take place, a transitional caretaker government must be instituted, composed of respected, trusted and skilled bureaucrats and supported by the military. The new transitional government should commit itself publicly to lay the grounds for systematic changes in all five categories and prepare the country for general elections in two years once a civil society is developed and political parties are organized. Any free but premature elections could lead to disastrous results because the winners at this stage may well be the extreme Islamic groups who are much better organized politically than any secular political parties and have been largely marginalized for decades.

To be sure, each nation in the region has its own specific characteristics and individual grievances. Tunisia has a strong secular and nationalist foundation that has enabled the revolution to be essentially devoid of Islamist elements. Others in the Arab world may not be so fortunate. In Egypt, the Muslim Brotherhood has largely assumed a more cautious approach for fear that their otherwise boisterous stand could lead to quick and violent retribution by the military. Undoubtedly, Islamists throughout the region will be looking to take advantage of the unrest gripping the region today, and the subsequent political upheaval. In Jordan, where unemployment officially rests at 14 percent (but where many believe the actual rate reaches 30 percent) the Muslim Brotherhood has already vowed to instigate protests "to demand improved living conditions as well as political and economic reforms."[2] Unlike Tunisia, Jordan lacks the secular or nationalist foundations that would seemingly guard against such Islamist influence. The same can be said of Yemen, the Arab world's poorest country, which is already gripped by civil war and is

2 "Jordan's Islamists vow more nationwide protests," *Ahram Online*, January 26, 2011, http://english. ahram.org.eg/NewsContent/2/8/4880/World/Region/Jordans-Islamists-vow-more-nationwide-protests.aspx.

home to al-Qaeda operatives directing attacks against the United States. Any Tunisia-style upheaval in such countries could lead to the kind of destabilizing chaos that would lead the region further away from the political freedoms that are being called for in the streets.

As suggested earlier, not every Arab state could or should follow the same roadmap for change. Nevertheless, each Arab leader should reassess their political reality and decide on a course of action that would allow them to shape the new order and yet be hailed as reformers rather than being forced out of office in disgrace. Every Arab king or Emir can gradually relinquish power to a Constructional Monarchy where the king or the Emir remains the head of the state and the prime minister is the head of the government with political powers mandated by a popularly elected parliament. The British or Swedish systems of government offer perfect examples. By following this path, current Arab Kings and Emirs can maintain the trappings of their positions as the heads of state, albeit with diminished powers, while at the same time meeting the people's demands and easing the transition of their countries into the inevitable change that will take place, come what may, either through upheaval and terrifying violence or through peaceful transition. The non-monarch Arab states may chose the Egyptian path allowing for gradual reforms, albeit under the watchful eyes of the military, to ensure stability and a peaceful transfer of power.

How soon the leaders of the Arab states take heed of what has happened in Tunisia and Egypt will determine not only their future but the future welfare and wellbeing of their peoples. No Arab leader should assume for a moment that they can somehow ride the revolutionary storm and maintain the status quo. The information revolutions may have triggered the revolution in Tunisia and Egypt but at this juncture with it or without it the wave of awakening is sweeping the Arab world. The leaders must now make their choice.

ALON BEN-MEIR

EGYPT—ISRAEL BILATERAL RELATIONS

ISRAEL AND EGYPT'S SHARED REGIONAL CONCERNS AND STRATEGIC INTERESTS WILL PRESERVE THE PEACE TREATY AND SHIELD THEIR BILATERAL RELATIONS

FEBRUARY 14, 2011

On Saturday, February 12, the Egyptian army issued a communiqué reassuring the Egyptian people and the international community of its intention to usher in a civilian government and honor all of Egypt's international commitments, including the peace treaty with Israel. Although such a pronouncement provided Israel with some comfort, many Israeli officials and ordinary citizens remain alarmed, perhaps for good reason, about the breathless development of events in Egypt and their mid and long-term implications on Israel and the Arab world. A careful analysis of these events strongly suggests, however, that the Egyptian military remains central to any future political development. Gauging the military's conduct and support of the 1979 Egyptian-Israeli peace treaty, it would appear that the military will continue to steadfastly safeguard the peace treaty not only because the army feels obligated, but because peace with Israel will continue to serve Egypt's national strategic interests.

There are four major pillars to this argument, and together they form the basis for maintaining and possibly improving Egyptian-Israeli bilateral relations, which opens up new opportunities for further advancing the Arab-Israeli peace process.

To better appreciate the Egyptian military's commitment to the Israeli-Egyptian peace treaty, it should be recalled that it was Egyptian General Anwar El-Sadat who forged peace with Israel in the wake of the 1973 Yom Kippur War. The ending of the 1973 war was rather unique as it was engineered by then-Secretary of State Henry Kissinger to allow Egypt to emerge politically triumphant by preventing the Israelis from crushing the Egyptian Third Army. Kissinger argued that another Egyptian defeat would only usher in the next war, and that Egypt, as the leader of the Arab world, must feel victorious and equal to the Israelis in order to come to the negotiating table. Allowing the military to remain in the Sinai at the conclusion of the hostilities was taken by the Egyptians, as it was intended to, as nothing less than a military victory which the Egyptian people continue to celebrate. This same peace treaty was steadfastly observed and further strengthened by Sadat's Vice President and successor, Hosni Mubarak, an Air Force General who became President following the assassination of Sadat.

This brief history between the two nations suggests four important implications. First, the Israeli-Egyptian peace treaty has been forged, sustained and somewhat institutionalized by military men and there is nothing to indicate that the current military leadership has any reason downgrade, let alone abrogate the treaty. Second, neither Israel nor Egypt has violated the agreement even once and both militaries have cooperated on a number of levels including intelligence sharing. Third, both countries have greatly benefited from the reduced military expenditure resulting from the substantial reduction in the state of military readiness against one another. Finally, considering the enormous efforts it would take to get Egypt out of its current political, social and economic doldrums, it would be at best foolish to renew hostilities with a neighbor in possession of formidable conventional military machine augmented with the reportedly fourth largest stockpile of nuclear weapons. In fact, if anything, the current Egyptian Military High Command looks favorably at the Egyptian peace treaty because it serves Egypt's greater strategic regional interests.

As the military listened to the public's demands, they also realized that the focus of the young revolutionaries was on their own plight—social and political freedom, economic opportunities, better health care, and education. The revolutionaries did not seek a scapegoat to blame for their dismal states of being; they did not blame Israel or the United States for their country's failures, and instead pointed the finger at their own leaders—the corruption and the stagnation from within. Here again, unlike many other Arabs who blame Israel, in particular, for all the ills that infect their society, the Egyptians appear to appreciate that peace with Israel as positive. Moreover, 70% of the Egyptian people were born since the peace treaty between Egypt and Israel was signed in 1979, and this majority of the population knows nothing but peace with Israel.

Whereas Mubarak has failed the Egyptian people by stifling social, economic and political developments, he has managed to ingrain the peace agreement with Israel in the national psyche of the Egyptian people. After all, peace was forged following a "military victory," and certainly not a defeat, a legacy that the military in particular wants to preserve. Even the Muslim Brotherhood vowed to keep the peace treaty with Israel should they assume power. Indeed, no revolution can make social, political and economic progress by becoming hostile to its neighbors, especially, in this case, Israel, with whom Egypt has no quarrel. Moreover, the Egyptian revolutionaries fully understood that each country looks after its own national interests, including Israel and the US, and it would have been up to the Egyptian authorities to look after the interest of the Egyptian people. The Arab malaise is bred from within, and to change it must also come from the strength, tenacity and will of the Egyptian people. It is in that sense that Egypt might again set an example to be emulated by the rest of the Arab states.

Both Israel and the Egyptian military—which is central in Egyptian politics—share common concerns over Islamic extremism. They have cooperated in the past and will continue to collaborate in the future. Although the Muslim Brotherhood may indeed be an entirely different breed than the Iranian hard core Islamists, and have professed to pursue political pluralism, both Israel and the Egyptian military remain suspicious of the Brotherhood's ultimate intentions. The influence of the Brotherhood on Hamas is significant, and neither Israel nor the Egyptian military see Hamas as a legitimate interlocutor as long as Hamas continues to reject the existence of Israel in principle.

It should be further noted that it was the Egyptian military, just as much as much as its Israeli counterpart, who kept tight control over the blockade of Gaza. Moreover, both the Israeli and Egyptian militaries are concerned over the rise of Islamic extremism altogether, a phenomenon that is not likely to dissipate following the Egyptian revolution. To be sure, depending on how the Egyptian revolution evolves, Egypt and Israel have far greater common interests than differences and the Egyptian military in particular is keenly aware of the potential gains and losses. In particular, the Egyptian army would like to maintain excellent relations with its US counterpart and continue to receive their over one billion dollars in military assistance. It would be impossible to maintain either should the Egyptian-Israeli peace treaty be undermined in any way.

Finally, what further cements future Egyptian-Israeli bilateral relations is the threat of Iran becoming a regional hegemon possibly equipped with nuclear weapons. Iran has been, and will remain, a major concern to both Israel and Egypt, and both countries have deep interests in preventing Iran from achieving its goals. Iran's growing influence in Iraq and the de facto takeover of Lebanon by Hezbollah only reinforce Israel and Egypt's concerns. For Egypt in particular, a nuclear Iran could overshadow Egypt's traditional leadership role in the Arab world and might even compel Egypt to pursue its own nuclear program. Neither prospect is attractive. Indeed, the last thing Egypt needs at this juncture is to enter into a nuclear race with Iran or continuously be threatened by Iran surrogates. Israel, on the other hand, while enjoying its own nuclear deterrence, wishes to prevent Iran from acquiring nuclear weapons not only out of fear that it would neutralize its own weapons, but because it could prevent other Arab states, especially in the Gulf, who would seriously be intimidated by Iran, from striking peace with Israel. Thus, Egypt and Israel have a very strong interest in preventing Iran from realizing its nuclear ambition. For Egypt and Israel, teaming together on this vitally important issue is of supreme importance to their national security. Egypt, in this particular case, looks at Israel as the bulwark that might eventually delay, if not stop, Iran's nuclear adventure, which adds another layer to their bilateral relationship.

The revolution in Egypt is a game changer in many ways and neither Egypt itself nor the Middle East will be the same again. That said, I believe that the Egyptian people in particular will stay the course of peace with Israel because the people's revolution is about internal social, political, and economic developments, and being free, productive and proud citizens. Maintaining the peace with Israel, under the guidance of the military, will help the young revolutionaries focus on their critical mission and reach their destination with dignity while knowing that their struggle has only just begun.

ALON BEN-MEIR

THE EGYPTIAN UPRISING: THE LESSON FOR ISRAEL

FEBRUARY 14, 2011

While much is unknown about the ultimate implications of the Egyptian uprising for Israel, one lesson can already be drawn: the missed opportunities to achieve peace with the Arab states could have disastrous impacts. Of course, many Israelis see the unraveling of the once-vaunted Egyptian government and argue that the increasingly precarious nature of the Arab regimes means that any peace agreement with them would be equally precarious. But rather than serve as an excuse not to make peace, the events in Egypt and the uncertainty they create for Israel should serve as a warning that missing opportunities to establish a status quo that offers Israel peace and security will instead lead to a status quo of regional instability, threats, and conflict.

Indeed, if Israel had accepted the Arab League's Peace Initiative and established normal relations with all 22 members, the anxiety that grips Israel with regard to the critical Israel-Egypt peace treaty would have been significantly diminished. Instead, today it must prepare for three possible scenarios: 1) an Egypt influenced greatly by the Muslim Brotherhood which rejects Israel in principle, 2) the establishment of a largely secular government, though not as friendly as the Mubarak government, or 3) a continuation of similar bilateral relations, since the Egyptian military has been behind the Israeli-Egyptian peace treaty. Because of the still-unfolding events, however, it can be assumed that any of the three scenarios could play out. Israel must therefore recalibrate its policies toward the Arab states because what happened in Tunisia, and especially Egypt, will impact other Arab countries in one way or another and the Middle East will never be the same.

The Muslim Brotherhood remains the only significantly organized opposition group in Egypt, strengthened by its network of social services provided throughout the country. While the Muslim Brotherhood is viewed as a political movement, it has served to influence and provide a common foundation for many Muslim extremists in the region, including its offshoot cousin, Hamas. Israel—rightly—is deeply concerned that the Brotherhood's head-start on other groups in political organization could allow it to have significant influence in a democratic Egypt—or even lead it. If the Brotherhood had such a prominent role in the largest and most influential Arab state, there would be fears of potential gains for Islamists in other nations, including in Jordan, Israel's most important neighbor. Such fears may include the possibility that Islamist Sunni and Shiite groups might coalesce around a common enemy, Israel, potentially gaining backing from Iran and unraveling the nascent support Israel has enjoyed from some Arab states in its efforts to stop Iran's nuclear pursuit. Furthermore, the possibility for a dramatic recalibration of Egyptian policy toward the Gaza Strip would require Israel to divert significant amounts of military resources to a border with Egypt that has been relatively calm for over thirty years. Plus, an end to the high level of intelligence cooperation with Egypt would require a great investment by Israel to keep tabs on a nation that was once hostile, but is now open, to engaging Islamist movements in the region. Finally, a hostile Egypt would likely cease the delivery of energy resources, which Israel has increasingly become dependent on to meet its needs.

These fears are already beginning to be expressed by Prime Minister Benjamin Netanyahu, who in his press conference with German Chancellor Angela Merkel indicated his concern that the Egyptian revolution could take the shape of the Iranian one in 1979. "Our real fear is of a situation that could develop ... and which has already developed in several countries including Iran itself—repressive regimes of radical Islam," he told reporters.[3] Meanwhile, many are pointing out that the uncertainty that now grips the Arab world makes peace agreements seemingly impossible to maintain with certainty, even with repressive dictators. The rise of influence of the Muslim Brotherhood in Egypt could exacerbate this anxiety, leaving Israel paralyzed while the status quo in the region crumbles around it.

The second more hopeful scenario from Israel's perspective would be the rise of a secular democratic Egypt that would maintain the peace treaty with Israel and good relations with the United States. The hope for this scenario *rests with the Egyptian army* and its desire to maintain a semblance of stability in the transition from the Mubarak regime to a truly democratic Egypt, void of significant influence from Islamists. Any new government would feel the impact of an end to the $1.5 billion in aid the United States sends to Egypt each year, largely as a result of the maintenance of the Egypt-Israel peace treaty. The Egyptian military has long maintained cooperation with Israel, keeping its forces out of the Sinai Peninsula and never violating the peace treaty—until Israel granted the Egyptian military permission to enter the Sinai during the protests of the past week. The prospect that Egypt's military would seek to maintain the aid it receives from the United States, while fully cooperating with the Pentagon as well as the intelligence cooperation it shares with Israel, provides hope that a democratic Egypt could eventually look more like Turkey than Iran.

That said, once the dust settles in Egypt and regardless of who or what political party or a coalition of parties rise to power, Israel should make it abundantly clear that it intends to observe and respect the bilateral peace agreement with Egypt. Israel should

---

3 Allyn Fisher-Ilan, "Israel's Netanyahu fears Egypt could go way of Iran," *Reuters,* last modified January 31, 2011. http://www.reuters.com/article/2011/01/31/us-israel-egypt-netanyahu-idUSTRE70U5L420110131.

invite the new Egyptian government to play a significant role, as Israel did its predecessors, in mediating between Israel and the Palestinians. Interestingly enough, throughout the uprising, Israel has not been particularly blamed for the Egyptian government's shortcomings, which may bode well for the future relations between the two countries.

Should Israel-Egypt and US-Egypt relations be largely maintained, Israel must still be concerned about the reverberations of the protests. Egypt's role as the center of Arab culture is likely to cause a wave of reform throughout the region. Other Arab leaders are already working to stay one step ahead of the waves of protest—King Abdullah of Jordan has dismissed his cabinet, including Prime Minister Samir Rifai, and Yemen's President Ali Abdullah Saleh declared he will not seek reelection nor will he hand power to his son when his term ends in 2013. To what extent such changes will satisfy the masses, and whether other governments will fall, remains to be seen.

In either scenario, Israel will need to be prepared to address a region in change. It will not be able to base its policies on the events happening in one country at a time; herein lies the opportunity of the current moment. In addition to seeking to maintain its peace with the newly shaped Egypt, Israel should also pursue bilateral tracks with Syria, the Palestinians and the Lebanese. Indeed, there is never truly an ideal moment to make peace; there will always be great uncertainty and a measure of risk. However, the risk of not achieving peace, or of achieving bilateral peace agreements which leave other conflicts unresolved, is simply unacceptable at a time when Israel is facing the rising threat of Islamic radicals, whether in the form of Iran to the east, Hamas to the south, or Hezbollah to the north.

The Arab League's peace initiative offers a way to mitigate risk and receive a maximum reward: normalized relations with its 22 nations. Indeed, the greater the number of Arab states with which it forges a peace agreement, the less threatened it will be. Should one Arab country violate such an agreement, it would be a violation of peace reached with all other Arab nations, not just Israel. The stakes, therefore, would be raised for all involved, and the resulting agreement would be all the more secure because of it.

Of course, whether the Arab Peace Initiative (API) itself will survive this period of turmoil remains to be seen. Israel should ensure that it does not miss the opportunity to utilize the Initiative once and for all. It can begin to do so by embracing the API, signaling its intention to engage Egypt and Jordan, the co-chairs of the Arab League's committee on the Arab Peace Initiative, and indicate its willingness to accept the principles of the Initiative as a basis for negotiations with the Palestinians and the Arab world at large. It must signal that it is prepared to support Egyptian democracy, work with the Egyptian government that is ultimately formed to maintain and even enhance Israel-Egypt relations, and, most importantly, meaningfully address the Palestinian question. Former Israeli Prime Minister Ehud Olmert and Palestinian Authority President Mahmoud Abbas came very close in 2008-2009 to forge an Israel-Palestinian accord; there is no reason why Israel, with the support of the Obama administration, should not resume negotiations from where they left off.

The Egyptian revolution has the potential for many great and positive developments, though of course there is always the possibility that the revolution may usher in a prolonged period of instability. Under any circumstances, Israel must remain focused on making peace and must invite the Egyptians to be an integral part of creating this peace. This would also send a powerful message that Israel is prepared to proactively establish a new, sustainable status quo in the Middle East based on peaceful relations and mutual security with all its neighbors.

Alon Ben-Meir

EGYPT'S NEWFOUND FOREIGN POLICY ASSERTIVENESS

MAY 31, 2011

Various Israeli and American officials and academics who have expressed concerns over Egypt's new foreign policy are misreading Cairo's intentions as well as the opportunities that a more confident and independent Egypt presents. The overthrow of former President Hosni Mubarak was driven by Egypt's domestic troubles—in particular its lack of political freedom and economic opportunity which must be systematically addressed for years to come. However, to meet the demands of its people, the new, more accountable Egyptian government will be driven to provide the kind of much-needed – and for many years sorely lacking – Arab leadership in the Middle East. Contrary to those who argue that the Mubarak government served to safeguard Western interests, it sat idle as the influence of non-Arab states like Turkey and Iran, and Islamist actors like Hamas and Hezbollah rose in a region barren of independence and opportunity. In this respect, a more assertive Egypt, providing Arab leadership, could emerge as a critical actor in support of regional security, stability and peace.

Rather than carry the mantle of Arab leadership as the leader of the most populated Arab state, President Hosni Mubarak's chief aim was the maintenance of his own regime. His ties with the United States and Israel - and the resulting American aid – were his chief tools in this regard. His clamping down on the Muslim Brotherhood also sought to achieve this same, single-minded goal. Meanwhile, Egypt's ties with key regional Arab nations like Syria, and non-Arab actors like Turkey and Iran, were frayed or seemingly non-existent. These policies and the breakdown in Egypt's foreign relations served to limit Egyptian influence in the region, even as it seemed to firmly entrench Mubarak's presidency. The result: while non-Arab actors like Turkey and Iran have wielded significant regional influence, Egypt virtually had none. While domestic considerations served to ignite Egypt's revolution, the lack of leadership only reinforced the image that President Mubarak's policies were contributing to the decline of the Arab world, rather than to its empowerment. The response by the Egyptian military following the explosion of protests throughout the country – to support and protect, rather than disperse the revolutionaries – suggested a tacit acknowledgement of this fact and provided it with an opportunity to establish a new, clean slate upon which to build. With Hosni Mubarak already at the advanced age of 82 and the possible succession of his son Gamal highly unpopular – along with the continuation of failed domestic and foreign policies – the military elite recognized that it was time to seize the opportunity to create much-needed change.

As the current Egyptian government stewards the nation in its transition to a more open and free democratic system, it has already begun to make the kind of domestic and foreign policy reforms that will be needed to re-assert Egyptian leadership. To be sure, it is understandable that the United States and Israel are troubled by data like the recent Pew Research poll indicating that 54 percent of Egyptians would like to see the Israel-Egypt peace treaty annulled and 79 percent have a negative view of the United States.[4] However, turning these figures around will require working with a new Egyptian government that is responsive to its people, not shunning or fearing them. Furthermore, privately and publicly, officials in the new Egyptian government and candidates for the Egyptian presidency have indicated their desire to demonstrate Egyptian leadership and independence, yet still abide by its treaty with Israel and maintain strategic ties with the United States to safeguard its own national security and economic interests. Abrogating the peace treaty with Israel would have tremendous political, economic and military repercussions that would kill any prospect of making progress in these areas and would quickly end Egypt's aspiration to resume its regional leadership role. In fact, in a recent interview with the Washington Post, the new Egyptian Foreign Minister Nabil Elaraby stated repeatedly that Egypt "made it very clear from the first day [of the new government] that we want to open a new page with all the countries in the world."[5] Regarding Egypt-U.S. ties, Elaraby said he expected them to be "stronger than ever," and in reference to Egypt-Israel ties he noted that "Egypt is going to comply with every agreement and abide by every treaty it has entered into."[6] Because of these assurances, the US and its European partners have made a significant additional economic aid package including debt relief to help Egypt jump-start its economic malaise.

Even so, Western fears of Egypt's new foreign policy direction are centered on three key concerns: the new government's outreach to the Muslim Brotherhood, Hamas, and Iran. The Muslim Brotherhood will undoubtedly play a key role in Egypt's future. Suppressing it proved unsuccessful under the Mubarak regime, and continuing to do so would be antithetical to the spirit of freedom and democracy, which drove the revolution. It is important to note that the Muslim Brotherhood did not lead the revolution. This was by-and-large a secular revolution seeking to expand the same kind of freedoms and opportunities that are enjoyed by the West. Furthermore, the Egyptian revolution was successful not by utilizing the violent tactics of Islamic extremists, but by peaceful protests in the streets. The new Egyptian government – and the Egyptian

4 "Egyptians Embrace Revolt Leaders, Religious Parties and Military, As Well," *Pew Research*, April 15, 2011. http://www.pewglobal.org/2011/04/25/chapter-4-relationship-with-the-united-states-and-israel/.

5 Lally Weymouth, "Egypt's foreign minister on the way forward after Mubarak," *Washington Post*, May 6, 2011. http://articles.washingtonpost.com/2011-05-06/opinions/35264382_1_fatah-and-hamas-palestinian-factions-unity-government.

6 Ibid.

military in particular – will not jeopardize the hope for a better future that has filled its citizens by enabling the Brotherhood to co-opt the revolution. Rather, creating progress toward greater regional leadership and expanded domestic opportunities will require the new government to co-opt the Brotherhood instead of suppressing and marginalizing it. If the new Egyptian government is to be responsive to its people, the new government must establish clear red lines with the Brotherhood, asserting that its participation in national politics is welcome, but as a political party dedicated to abiding by the political process, not as sect of Islamist revolutionaries. Moreover, for the Egyptian government to undertake significant social and economic development programs it will have to include the Brotherhood, which enjoys popularity in these two spheres. A greater political role for the Muslim Brotherhood will translate into greater responsibility for the group, and with that responsibility comes accountability, moderation, and compromise. As such, the inclusion of the Muslim Brotherhood will be an important component in establishing a relationship between religion and state that is uniquely suited to Egyptian society, still under the wrathful eyes of the military.

The Hamas-Fatah reconciliation agreement is the first indication of the prospect for a stronger, more influential post-Mubarak Egypt. A conflict that Mubarak's government had been mediating for years was concluded by the new Egyptian government in less than three months. On Mubarak's watch, the absence of influential Arab leadership indirectly enabled violent conflicts to fester between Israel and Hezbollah, and Israel and Hamas. Already, under the nascent Hamas-Fatah unity deal, Hamas has indicated its willingness to allow Mahmoud Abbas to negotiate with Israel regarding a Palestinian state in the West Bank and Gaza, and pledged as a part of the reconciliation agreement not to use violence.

The Mubarak government's strained relationship with Hamas, the Brotherhood's offshoot in Gaza, effectively handcuffed Egypt from playing a meaningful role in moderating Hamas' position or mediating Israeli-Palestinian disputes. While Egypt's overtures to Hamas and its opening of the Egypt-Gaza border may be troubling to Israel, Egypt's interests remain to maintain stability and security along its borders, especially with Israel, while distancing Hamas from Syria and Iran. Indeed, to protect its own national security interests, Egypt would be foolish to allow the smuggling of weapons to Hamas through the newly open crossing. A new Israeli-Hamas conflagration would severely undercut Egypt's new policy initiative. Moreover, the opening of the Rafah crossing between Gaza and Egypt would ease the international pressure on Israel over its blockade of Gaza while increasing Egypt's control over the Strip. Indeed, an Egypt that is better positioned to work with Hamas is one that is more likely to succeed in moderating Hamas' positions, in halting rocket fire on Israel, and even in securing the release of captured Israeli Cpl. Gilad Shalit.

The potential for Egypt to serve as a diplomatic conduit is also promising with regard to its renewed ties with Iran. As Amr Moussa, the Secretary General of the Arab League and a leading candidate for Egypt's presidency told the Washington Post recently, "Iran is not the natural enemy of Arabs, and it shouldn't be. We have a lot to gain by peaceful relations — or less tense relations — with Iran."[7] Egypt does not need to be Iran's enemy, but it is a natural competitor. If Egypt is to provide leadership in the Arab world, its ability to maintain dialogue and influence with nations across the region, from Israel to Iran, will be critical. Just as Egypt can benefit from its burgeoning ties with Hamas and the Muslim Brotherhood, talks between Egypt and Iran offer an opportunity to better gauge Iran's nuclear intentions and might even place Egypt in a better position than Turkey to mediate Tehran's disputes with the West. While working to moderate Iran's behavior is for the betterment of the entire region, no country is better positioned than Egypt to also warn Iran of the potentially catastrophic consequences of continuing to threaten Israel existentially.

Finally, what further concerns the United States and Israel is how these new initiatives will play out and what might be the next step that Egypt will take. The answer to these questions is that a stronger, more assertive, and more democratic Egypt that seeks to advance its own interests could also further the interests it continues to share with the United States and Israel: security and peace throughout the Middle East. Certainly, the new Egypt will need time to develop its new regional posture. However, rather than view Egypt's newfound assertiveness and independence as a threat, officials in Washington and Jerusalem should view the new Egyptian leadership as providing an important opportunity to improve relations with the Arab world on the path toward achieving these long-elusive goals.

7 Lally Weymouth, "Amr Moussa's vision for Egypt," *Washington Post*, May 9, 2011. http://articles.washingtonpost.com/2011-05-09/opinions/35232481_1_parliamentary-elections-egypt-presidential-elections.

ALON BEN-MEIR

IS THIS WHAT THE REVOLUTION WAS ALL ABOUT?

SEPTEMBER 19, 2011

The great promises of the Egyptian revolution appear to be dissipating into a chaotic state of disorder, shattering the prospect of a new democratic and progressive Egypt serving as a model to the rest of the Arab world. The Supreme Council of the Armed Forces is failing miserably to balance populism with responsible governance and regional leadership. Egypt today appears to be a floundering state with a transitional government that is rapidly losing legitimacy in the eyes of its people and losing credibility in the eyes of the international community.

Security has been a major concern for Israel since the fall of Hosni Mubarak, a long and trusted ally of the US and Israel. The terror attacks in Southern Israel and Israel's killing of Egyptian policemen in the Sinai enraged Israeli and Egyptian masses alike, plunging the Egyptian-Israeli peace treaty into doubt like never before. Just more than a week after an Egyptian mob tore down the Israeli flag from the Israeli Embassy in Cairo, on September 10 the walls of the compound were breached and a mob ransacked the embassy, threatening the lives of the Israeli personnel inside.[8] For Egyptian security forces to allow this to occur is inexcusable under any circumstances. It was more than obvious that momentum was building for this attack and yet internal security forces sat on their hands doing little to prevent such an egregious violation of diplomatic protocol and Egypt's international obligation to protect foreign embassies.

The repercussions of the Egyptian governments' failure of leadership will affect more than its bilateral relations with Israel. It will leave a terrible impression on many other nations, especially the United States and the European Union, on which Egypt so heavily depends. The haphazard nature of the embassy episodes portray a nation in utter turmoil, and a government that is seeking to placate angry mobs in the name of democracy while presumably fulfilling its international responsibilities. It is clear that the interim Egyptian government must choose a clear and cohesive policy, and not merely react to the mob's demands. Until it does, the international community will not have confidence in Egypt to serve as a trustworthy regional partner.

The Egyptian authorities are not likely to allow the peace treaty with Israel to collapse, but through their negligence the relationship could deteriorate to a point where a single event could lead to a total collapse. What would happen if, under pressure, Hamas

---

8 "Crowds attack Israel embassy in Cairo," *Al Jazeera*, September 10, 2011, http://www.aljazeera.com/news/middleeast/2011/09/201199225334494935.html.

provoked Israel into another war in Gaza? How would the Egyptian government respond to popular rage then? The upcoming vote on Palestinian statehood at the United Nations, and the expected protests in its wake, could lead to Egypt's first test in this regard. Meanwhile, in the U.S. Congress, further reports of the strain on Israel-Egypt ties will inevitably lead to greater populist calls for ending aid to Egypt altogether, exactly at a time when it needs the support of the international community to rebuild a battered nation.

Although the transitional government is not supposed to make major foreign policy initiatives but instead serve as a caretaker government until a new one is elected, this government has shifted significantly on major foreign policy issues by seeking to align itself with its traditional rivals, Turkey and Iran. During his visit this week to Egypt, Turkish Prime Minister Recep Tayyip Erdogan delivered a verbal attack on Israel, further fermenting anti-Israeli sentiments on Egyptian soil with the blessing of its government while signing trade agreements to triple commercial ties with Egypt, in an effort to appeal to the Egyptian street.

Furthermore, Egyptian authorities continue to downplay the historical rivalry between Egypt and Iran. Last February 2011, the Egyptian Authority agreed to allow two Iranian war ships to pass through the Suez Canal to the Mediterranean heading for Syria. In each case these niceties were not based on any structural foundation of strategic interests and are unlikely to last. If Egypt is to regain regional leadership, it will inevitably resume its role as a rival of both Ankara and Tehran. The last thing the Arab world and Egypt in particular wants is a return to Ottoman-style Turkish dominance or to succumb to Iran's ambition to become a regional hegemon with nuclear weapons capabilities.

At the same time, the Arab Gulf states have become increasingly concerned with Cairo's posturing. As the nations of the Gulf search for ways to reach a better understanding with Israel over their growing concerns regarding Iran, Egypt is undermining the Sunni Arab alliance. Instead of proposing a coherent foreign policy, the Egyptian government is using Israel as a political football to distract and placate the masses in the short-term, at the expense of its long-term interests.

More than eight months into the revolution, there is still no sign of where Egypt is going in terms of social and economic development. Mubarak was deposed, but his colleagues remain in power with different names and titles. Thus, it is no surprise that many of the same problems remain. People need jobs, education, health care and a real prospect for better days to come. What has this government done to advance a new socio-economic and political order? Today, doctors, airport employees, and engineers have gone on strike, and thousands of teachers and students have demonstrated in the streets.

The government has cracked down on media freedom and reports indicate that Egyptian women are being increasingly sidelined from political participation. Instead of developing at a minimum a two-year plan to lay the foundation for new socio-economic initiatives to create jobs and meet some of the public basic needs, Egypt is floundering, headed for an election for which the newly emerging political parties are not prepared. The public dialogue with these parties is limited and the Muslim Brotherhood could win more than a third of the new parliament. Maybe this is exactly what the military junta wants—a cozy deal with the Brotherhood as long as the military can maintain its supreme authority over national security, foreign policy issues, and its vast economic enterprises. Is this what Egyptians really want and what the revolution was all about?

As a supporter of Egypt and admirer of its people, it pains me to see Egypt's transitional rulers gambling with the nation's future. The hope that Egypt can emerge from its transition from dictatorship to a secure, stable and prosperous democracy is increasingly dim, to the detriment of the people of Egypt and the entire region.

THE EGYPTIAN REVOLUTION: A YEAR LATER

JANUARY 25, 2012

Many observers and analysts of the Arab Spring have tended to draw quick conclusions about the successes or failures of the revolutionary upheavals that have swept the Middle East and North Africa based on what has thus far transpired on the ground. This is a common mistake. Every Arab country that has gone through the revolution remains immersed within the very early stages of the revolutionary process. To determine the real prospects for political and economic reforms in any of these countries, we have to look into the nature of the grassroots movements that precipitated the revolution, the core issues that the newly-emerging governments face, and the choices they are likely to make. Looking at Egypt from this perspective reveals that, notwithstanding the continuing political squabbles and the combined margins of victory of the Islamic parties in the new parliament, the country is on a path of real political recovery, however long this process may take.

There are two opposing views of the current situation in Egypt that appear to dominate the present discourse a year after the revolution that successfully toppled President Hosni Mubarak. The first, which I dub the "nothing changed" view, assesses that not much change has occurred in the country's socio-political and economic landscape. For proponents of this view, the regime did not fall – only its head did – specifically because the military regime that has been ruling Egypt since Gamal Abdel Nasser's coup in 1952 is still in charge, keeping the country's power structure and institutions essentially intact. From the perspective of those who subscribed to the view of "Mubarak-or-chaos," the survival of this regime has alienated the secular revolutionary forces while empowering political Islam. Moreover, it has also brought real chaos to the daily lives of Egyptians, ranging from chronic crises in the provisions of basic goods, to high crime rates and uncertainty about the country's transitional roadmap.

The second view, the so-called "everything changed" view, is shared mostly by those who hold an anti-Islamist posture including a plethora of secular Arab groups, many conservative or reform-minded constituencies in the United States and Europe, the Israeli government and others, and insists that Egypt has undergone an irreversible change towards religious extremism. For them, the advent of Islamic forces will allow the Muslim Brotherhood (MB), along with the ultra-extremist Salafist groups (who control over almost 70% of Egypt's legislature), to draft the country's constitution, which would likely adopt Sharia law.[9] In addition, their sweeping popularity will also

---

9 "Egypt assembly votes on constitution," *BBC News*, November 29, 2012, http://www.bbc.co.uk/news/world-middle-east-20536323.

allow them to decide Egypt's presidency. For the believers in this view, Islamic forces are aggressive, anti-West, and anti-Israel. An MB-dominated government in Cairo is likely to reverse the strategic alliance with the United States as well as the peace treaty with Israel, renew the domestic conflict, and join the region's Iran-led extremist axis, along with Syria, Hezbollah, and Hamas.

I cannot disagree more with these two views. They are misguided, and the pessimism they convey is misleading and potentially dangerous. There are three major reasons for my optimism about Egypt's revolution and its future.

First, the Egyptian military will remain a powerful player in Egyptian politics and will not yield its role as the guardian of Egypt's national security interests. Though this might look as a validation of the "nothing changed" view, what constitutes a revolution if not the electoral victory of the oppressed opposition group under the old regime in the country's fairest and freest election in ages? What took place in Egypt is by all measures a *revolution*, but like any other revolution it cannot be perfect and produce immediate and comprehensive success. To enact the aims of the revolution, it needs an evolutionary process (which is currently going on) through which it will eventually find its way. As the traditional Egyptian saying goes, *el-Sabr Tayyeb* – patience is sweet, especially for a country that is known for its stamina, wit, and long, unbroken history.

The continuing involvement of the Egyptian military in the political process remains central to the future health of the country's political development, and for good reason. As the sole institution that remained cohesive after the revolution, it has the ability to pave the road and secure a more peaceful state of affairs, unlike the chaotic situation that prevailed in Iran in 1979 following the collapse of all government bodies. In addition, due to its vast economic empire and its vested interest in maintaining the peace with Israel and the flow of U.S. military and economic aid, the Egyptian military is in a perfect position to counter any extremist, confrontational approaches that might emerge, though unlikely, from the elected parliament that the Islamist parties dominate. In fact, the MB and the military have already reached an understanding that offers immunity for some of the military high brass and the preservation of the military's privileges. The two sides have also agreed that the Parliament will choose a prime minister to run the country's domestic affairs, including education, healthcare, and economic development, and a President, to be elected by a popular vote to oversee foreign policy and national security matters.

Second, the MB is a rational and realistic actor, and several factors attest to this fact. The MB will continue its non-violent approach, which it adopted several decades ago and brought them to this point. They have committed themselves to the preservation of the peace treaty with Israel while counseling Hamas to be less confrontational with the Jewish state. The MB leadership offered to share power with secular forces in the new parliament and signed a declaration that was put forward by Al-Azhar, the Center of Sunni Islamic learning, that would protect theological dissent, freedom of religious observance, scientific inquiry, and artistic expression.[10]

It appears that the MB is fully cognizant and appreciative of the real sentiments of the people that brought them to this stage. Why then would they change course and lose everything they have gained? They have heard loud and clear the public grievances and outcries of those young men and women who yearn for dignity and freedom, and gave them the political power to secure these basic rights. They want jobs, they want education, they want health care, they want an opportunity to live and prosper, and they want freedom. They did not go to Tahrir Square demanding the destruction of Israel. They have heard and seen enough excuses from Arab countries that use Israel as the incarnation of the devil and blame it for all of their shortcomings while the people continue to suffer with disdain.

Third, the Egyptian revolution has certainly removed the Egyptian citizen's psychological barrier of fearing the government and its internal security apparatus, which has existed for so long. In addition to the fact that millions made their way to their country's fairest and freest elections in decades, the revolution has activated the power of young Egyptian men and women to be engaged in political activism, volunteer work, and business. As Ahmed Assam, a young Egyptian software engineer put it, "the Revolution created a feeling that people can change the world for the better."[11] Equally important is that the plethora of Egypt's media outlets are replete with voices of criticism and sarcasm towards the country's chronic problems as well as the policies of almost every single political actor. No party or institution has been immune from criticism and review, including the military council and its head Field Marshal Hussein Tantawi, the government, the MB, and all other parties.

Bloggers and social media members can easily mobilize demonstrations of millions in Tahrir Square and elsewhere in Egypt. It is this unprecedented ability of the Egyptian people to transform their country while maintaining their incredible sense of humor that will prevent whoever comes to power from reverting to dictatorship or imposing archaic Islamic laws and once again subjecting the people to a police state which trumps civil and political rights with impunity. The Egyptian youth now know where the real power rests and they have no intention of ever relinquishing what they have gained after decades of quiet desperation.

10 David D. Kirkpatrick, "In Egypt, Signs of Accord Between Military Council and Islamists," *The New York Times*, January 22, 2012, http://www.nytimes.com/2012/01/23/world/middleeast/signs-of-accord-between-egyptian-military-and-muslim-brotherhood-on-new-charter.html?pagewanted=all&_r=0.
11 Andrew Torchia, "Egypt entrepreneurs see new dawn post-Revolution," *Reuters*, January 18, 2012. http://www.reuters.com/article/2012/01/18/us-egypt-entrepreneurs-idUSTRE80H1LL20120118.

The United States and its allies, especially Israel, must accept the fact that in the wake of the Arab Spring, Islamic governments are likely to dominate the Arab political landscape. This does not suggest that these governments will follow Iran's model and naturally commit themselves to hostility toward the West or seek Israel's destruction. Without throwing caution to the wind, the US and its allies will be wise to adopt a proactive policy toward Egypt. They must demonstrate that they stand for democracy, in words and in deeds, and welcome any genuine democratic development in Egypt that leads to sustainable reforms and progress, however treacherous the road may be.

EGYPT CAN RISE TO THE HISTORICAL OCCASION BUT IT MUST CHOOSE WISELY

MARCH 5, 2012

A few days after the Egyptian uprising, I argued that the Arab Spring could well turn into a long and cruel winter due to a host of prominent factors including the lack of traditional liberalism, the elites' control of business, a military that clings to power, and the religious divide and Islamic extremism. These factors are making the transformation into a more reformist governance slow, filled with hurdles and punctuated with intense violence, much to the chagrin of Utopian-minded Western governments who thought that the transition to democracy would be attainable within months. If and when the Muslim Brotherhood (MB) and the ruling Military Council reach a power-sharing agreement, the situation will continue to unravel and be punctuated by chaos and accompanied by violence.

A testimony to this chaos is the recent crisis over the democracy-promoting U.S. NGOs working in Egypt. In a classic case of diversionary policies, the military-led government attempted to divert the attention of the public away from the worsening economic and security conditions by putting 19 U.S. citizens on trial for illegally working in Egypt for NGOs that receive unregistered foreign funding.[12] U.S. threats to cut off the $1.3 billion in aid to the military resulted in the release of its citizens a few days ago. Left confused as to what this fuss was all about, the Egyptian public reacted sharply against the military, accusing it of being too incompetent to run the country's affairs. While this does not suggest that the Egyptian revolution or the Arab Spring is doomed, it does offer a reminder to those young men and women who seek a promising future that they must remain armed with determination, prudence and the courage to act when a change of course is needed yet again.

To set the path for future democratic stability in Egypt, a resuming of the country's leadership role in the Arab world and carefully considered regional responsibilities, any new Egyptian government needs to follow a number of steps:

First, the electorally-triumphant Islamic parties should not be tempted to exercise hegemony, but should rather push for pluralism ensuring that any government is representative, in word and deed, of Egypt's wide political spectrum. Demonstrating prudence,

---

12 Amro Hassan, "19 Americans to stand trial in Egypt on Feb. 26," *Los Angeles Times*, February 18, 2012, http://latimesblogs.latimes.com/world_now/2012/02/foreign-ngo-workers-to-be-tried-on-feb26.html.

the MB has decided to distance itself from a coalition with the ultra-conservative Salafi party and has instead sought out an agreement with the liberal parties.13 However, there is a growing concern among Egypt's democrats that the MB will use their sugar-coated coalition with the liberals to hide their real intentions: to gradually "Islamize" the country's institutions and society instead of working on the desperately-needed socioeconomic reforms. The policies that the new government will pursue and to what extent it will embrace pluralism will signal to the Egyptian people not only how it is responding to their needs, but will also send a clear message to the Arab world as to where Egypt is actually heading. The Arab youth do not want their or any other Arab government to be fashioned after the Iranian regime, and will rise again if they feel betrayed.

Second, the new government should embark on extensive sustainable development projects to revive the economy. To some, the economic gloom might seem to be lifting in Egypt, but they must remember that this "brighter" prospect is mainly due to the $3.2 billion loan the government expects to sign shortly with the International Monetary Fund in the hopes that this will clear the way for other foreign aid.[14] However, foreign aid can only solve immediate and not long-term economic problems and no foreign aid-dependent country is likely to become prosperous. Egypt's current dismal economic reality can only be solved through sustainable development strategies, which depend on decentralized decision-making on economic projects and the transfer of managerial authority, skills, and capacities to sub-national levels, all of which are key to advancing democracy and development from the bottom-up.

Decided on by the local communities and funded by micro-finance loans, these development projects will help alleviate the country's endemic poverty, create jobs, and empower the masses, particularly women. Islamic parties can be a natural ally to this form of economic development, not only because the majority of their activities have historically been providing social services at the grassroots level, but also because this model identifies with the Islamic concepts of *Shura* (consultation) and *Ijma* (consensus-building). Instead of responding to a recent call from the prominent Salafi preacher Mohamed Hassan for citizens to raise money to do away with US aid,[15] wealthy Egyptians should donate towards this type of development. Knowing the experience of Bangladesh and Morocco, substantial donations will get a significant return and help advance the country's economic and democratic prospects.

13 David D. Kirkpatrick, "In Egypt, No Alliance With Ultraconservatives, Islamist Party Says," *The New York Times*, December 1, 2011. http://www.nytimes.com/2011/12/02/world/middleeast/egypts-muslim-brotherhood-keeps-distance-from-salafis.html?_r=1&.
14 Tom Pfeiffer, "Analysis: Economic gloom begins to lift in Egypt," *Reuters*, February 29, 2012. http://www.reuters.com/article/2012/02/29/us-egypt-economy-idUSTRE81S12T20120229.
15 "Egyptians launch fundraising campaigns to abolish US aid," *Egypt Independent*, February 14, 2012. http://www.egyptindependent.com/news/egyptians-launch-fundraising-campaigns-abolish-us-aid.

Third, the new government (with a significant MB component) should maintain peace with Israel as a pillar of Egypt's national security. In a panel discussion I participated in with *al-Hurra* last month, which included the General Secretary of the MB's Freedom and Justice Party (FJP), Mahmoud Hussein, it was stated by Hussein that the FJP would honor the peace but is not really interested in talking with the Israelis. Also, in the midst of the American NGO crisis in Egypt, the FJP countered the U.S. threat to cut aid to the country by threatening to review the peace treaty with Israel.[16] These are worrying signs as they ignore the major outcry from the Egyptian and other Arab revolutionaries who were spurred by domestic failures and deprivations, not by hatred and disdain toward Israel. The revolutionaries did not burn Israeli flags and call for "death to Israel" but instead demanded freedom, opportunity and dignity. The MB seems to treat the peaceful relations with Israel as if they are doing Israel a favor, when in fact the peace is in Egypt's own national interest. The preservation of the peace will prevent another deliberate or accidental armed confrontation, which would heavily tax the Egyptian economy. Egypt would have to allocate tens of billions of dollars towards a war with Israel, which it does not have, while losing U.S. financial assistance without any prospect of challenging Israel militarily. And to what end? Israel is an unmitigated reality and the Egyptian people can benefit greatly from normal relations from a technologically and economically-advanced neighboring country.

Finally, any new government should aggressively pursue a restoration of Egypt's regional role. Though poor in resources, Egypt has always been the epicenter of the Arab world, and the model that emerges in Egypt will certainly have an impact on the entire Middle East. But for the Egyptians to set an example for the rest of the Arab world, they will have to take the lead in the Arab Spring revolutions. Thus far, unfortunately, the military-led government has chosen to remain an observer in Libya, Syria, and Yemen. It has even allowed Iranian ships to cross the Suez Canal en route to Syria carrying arms to the Assad regime,[17] which he uses to suppress and kill his people who, like their Egyptian counterparts, simply seek to be free. For political, security and geo-strategic reasons, the new government in Egypt cannot afford to lose Egypt's traditional leadership role in the Arab world by allowing a small Arab country like Qatar to take the lead or permitting Iran to rise to the position, a country that is lying in wait to usurp the political and regional agenda.

16 David D. Kirkpatrick, "Egyptian Party Threatens to Review Treaty With Israel," *The New York Times*, February 16, 2012, http://www.nytimes.com/2012/02/17/world/middleeast/muslim-brotherhood-threatens-to-review-peace-treaty-with-israel.html.
17 "'Iranian warships arrive at Syrian port,'" *Jerusalem Post*, February 18, 2012. http://www.jpost.com/IranianThreat/News/Article.aspx?id=258368.

Neither the Egyptian people nor the international community should expect a smooth transition from dictatorship to democracy. But the new government in Cairo should work, in cooperation with its regional and international partners, to smooth the transitional process and shorten the period of chaos and instability, which will lead to sustained democratic reforms (albeit with Islamic values). Egypt *can* rise to the historic occasion but it must now choose wisely.

ISRAEL AND THE MUSLIM BROTHERHOOD: FACING THE BITTER-SWEET REALITY

MARCH 12, 2012

Since the fall of the Mubarak regime, the conventional wisdom in Israel has suggested that an Islamist government in Egypt would necessarily be hostile to the Jewish state. Egypt's parliamentary elections, in which the Muslim Brotherhood (MB) won close to 50 percent of the vote, only reinforced this notion, which Prime Minister Netanyahu viewed with a suspicious "wait-and-see" attitude. On its part, the MB's Freedom and Justice Party (FJP) seems equally unwilling to change their posture towards what they still call the "Zionist entity." That both sides are loath to talk to one another not only ignores the hardcore realities on the ground but also deepens pre-existing misperceptions.

Israel and the MB should accept the fact that they exist and will continue to exist in the same neighborhood indefinitely regardless of their feelings or beliefs about each other. Moreover, by accepting the inevitability of their mutual realities, Israel and the MB can and should cooperatively bring an end to the Israeli-Palestinian conflict which is central to improving Israeli-Egyptian bilateral relations and remains the cornerstone of regional stability.

Representing nearly 50 percent of the Egyptian people, the MB is likely to form the new government and relies on an almost unbreakable organizational structure in control of a vast socioeconomic network deeply entrenched in society.[18] This is not necessarily bad news for Israel as the MB has consistently shown moderation in their overall political strategy.

Domestically, the MB is negotiating with the military to reach a power-sharing agreement and continues to move forward with its non-violent approach, which they adopted several decades ago and has led them to where they are today. The MB leadership has offered to form a coalition with secular parties in the new parliament and has deliberately refrained from nominating a candidate of their own for the presidency to avoid the impression that they are the dominant powerhouse, which also carries a heavy responsibility which they do not want to shoulder at this juncture.

---

18 Eric Trager, "The Unbreakable Muslim Brotherhood," *Foreign Affairs*, September/October 2011. http://www.foreignaffairs.com/articles/68211/eric-trager/the-unbreakable-muslim-brotherhood.

Internationally, the MB has committed itself to maintaining the peace treaty with Israel and cooperating with the United States.[19] The MB and the Arab world's Islamic parties are large and from every indication they are not likely to become another Islamic Republic à la Iran, albeit political Islam *will* be a part of any political system that may emerge. To be sure, the MB and Iran simply do not see eye to eye. Their bilateral relations will, at best, be based on mutual suspicion. In fact, the chairman of the Foreign Affairs committee in the Egyptian parliament, FJP member Dr. Essam al-Arian, recently stated ominously that the Arab Spring would also reach Iran.[20]

With the continuing impasse between Israel and the Palestinians and considering the immense influence that the MB exerts on Hamas, the MB could certainly become an important interlocutor between Israel and the Palestinians, particularly since Israeli-Palestinian peace will be impossible without Hamas. The MB has a vested interest in maintaining the calm along the Israeli-Gaza border. Egypt's recent success in negotiating a ceasefire between Israel and Islamic Jihad only confirms Egypt's significant role in this regard—a role that Cairo has repeatedly played in the past to prevent escalation of violence. Indeed, should serious violent conflict occur between Israel and Hamas, the MB, as it forms the new government, cannot come to the aid of Hamas and risk a confrontation with Israel, or ignore the Egyptian people's outcry should Israel conduct a major onslaught against Gaza. Moreover, the MB cannot tamper with the diplomatic relations with Israel without undermining the peace treaty, nor can it afford to ignore calls by the newly elected People's Assembly (the Parliament) requesting the government to recall the Egyptian ambassador in Tel Aviv and expel the Israeli ambassador in Cairo, in protest of the "Israeli aggression" on Gaza.

Israel might find it easier to deal with the Egyptian military, which has been ruling the country since the coup of 1952. However, the fact that the military itself has yielded to the reality of the MB suggests a significant change in the role of the military in Egyptian politics, especially in light of the fact that the rise of Islamic parties will play a significant, if not dominant, role in the wake of the Arab Spring. Realpolitik aside, Israel has to reconcile itself with the fact that the MB has come to power through a democratic process and Israel would be wise to accept who the Egyptians have elected in their first free and fair elections in the country's history. The MB can exert the greatest moderating influence over Hamas to accept Israel's reality and facilitate peace negotiations between the two sides, as they have abandoned violence and accepted the peace with Israel. To be sure, the MB can serve both as a facilitator and a model.

19 "Senator John Kerry and U.S. Ambassador Visit FJP, Discuss Egypt's Democratic Transition," *Ikhwan Web*, December 10, 2011. http://www.ikhwanweb.com/article.php?id=29395.
20 Zvi Bar'el, "Muslim Brotherhood lawmaker: Arab Spring headed to Iran," *Haaretz*, February 28, 2012. http://www.haaretz.com/news/middle-east/muslim-brotherhood-lawmaker-arab-spring-headed-to-iran-1.415380.

Israel should also recognize the MB leadership as a legitimate and integral part of the Egyptian political body. Immediately after the uprising of the Egyptians in February 2011, Israel's former ambassador in Cairo, Yitzhak Levanon, had requested permission from his superiors in the Foreign Ministry to establish a dialogue with the MB – much like the United States and several European countries.[21] It was no surprise that the ambassador's useful request was rejected by Israeli Foreign Minister Lieberman. This attitude only adds further to Israel's estrangement in the eyes of the MB, the de-facto future governing authority. Indeed, how could any Israeli concern over the MB possibly be addressed without attempting dialogue?

To test the MB resolve and willingness to facilitate an Israeli-Palestinian peace accord, Israel should convey to the MB its readiness to provide general parameters of a two-state solution. In addition, Israel should further convey its preparedness to engage Hamas, along with the Palestinian Authority, in negotiations once Hamas follows in the Palestinian Authority's footsteps by formally and permanently abandoning violence as a means to achieve the Palestinians' national objective of statehood.

Although the MB has come to terms with the existence of Israel in the Middle East, this acceptance should now transcend a reluctant commitment to maintaining the already cold peace between Egypt and Israel to a dialogue on a wider spectrum of issues. As I argued in a recent article,[22] Egypt must engage in sustainable development projects to overcome its current dismal economic reality. Having established a state with an outstanding economic success based on sustainable development and technological breakthroughs, Israel is perhaps Egypt's best partner in this regard, not to mention the possibilities of cooperation in the areas of education, irrigation technology, and foreign investment.

Israel should capitalize on the MB's ascendance to power in Egypt to facilitate the engagement of Hamas and other Palestinian Islamic groups in the peace process. The sooner Israeli-Palestinian peace is achieved, the wider the door will open for coexistence and cooperation between Israel and the Islamic forces that will dominate the Arab world for years to come.

21 Eli Brdnstein, "'We should encourage dialogue' with the Muslim Brotherhood," *Ma'ariv*, December 18, 2011. http://www.nrg.co.il/online/1/ART2/317/256.html.
22 See "Egypt Can Rise to the Historical Occasion But It Must Choose Wisely," page 47.

TO EGYPT'S YOUTH: THE REVOLUTION
IS STILL YOURS TO RECLAIM

APRIL 23, 2012

In the past few weeks, the Egyptian revolutionary youth's worst nightmare has come to pass: they have been caught in a horrifying struggle between the *old regime* and the Islamists amidst chaos in every aspect of Egyptian life. Before the transitional period deadline of June 30 of this year, the Muslim Brotherhood (MB) and the ruling Supreme Council of the Armed Forces (SCAF) (once thought to have reached a power-sharing understanding) are squabbling as to who will have the upper hand after the transition. The secular forces, meanwhile, are divided over every single aspect of the political process, all amidst a crushing economic crisis that risks the bankrupting the country.[23]

At stake is the survival of the revolution itself. Egypt's youth should re-take the lead (as they courageously did in January 2011) and form a unified front to usurp from politicians ownership of the country's transitional process to democracy, and ensure the achievement of its central aims: "food, freedom, and social justice."

Ostensibly intoxicated with its landslide electoral victory, the MB broke its earlier promise not to monopolize the political process, attempted to dictate the makeup of the constitutional assembly, and nominated a presidential candidate in the elections scheduled for next month. But the judiciary, suspected to be under SCAF influence, disqualified both the constitutional assembly as well as the MB's principal presidential candidate, Khairat El-Shater, along with others, including former intelligence chief Omar Suleiman, whose candidacy was anathema to the MB and the public at large. The MB is still running an alternate candidate, Dr. Mohamed Morsi, and appears ready to defame the victory of any other as a "forgery".[24] In the meantime, the SCAF is tacitly communicating its readiness to dissolve the parliament or even delay the presidential elections altogether if an agreement is not reached on drafting the new constitution that would ensure the independence of the military decision-making and the budget.

---

23 Damien McElroy, "Egypt 'needs £7.5 billion bail-out to avoid bankruptcy,'" *The Telegraph*, April 16, 2012. http://www.telegraph.co.uk/news/worldnews/africaandindianocean/egypt/9207426/Egypt-needs-7.5-billion-bail-out-to-avoid-bankruptcy.html.
24 Marwa Awad and Abdel Rahman Youssef, "Exclusive: Mubarak aide presidency bid an "insult": Islamist rival," *Reuters*, April 8, 2012, http://www.reuters.com/article/2012/04/08/us-egypt-brotherhood-idUSBRE8370C220120408.

As the two titans clash, the secular forces appear to be in disarray and more divided than ever. The liberals' favorite, Mohamed Elbaradei, has withdrawn his presidential candidacy. The efforts by the Committee of 100, the self-appointed group of prominent figures from Egypt's elite,[25] to convince those presidential contenders not from the *old regime* to form a single team have failed, while several revolutionary forces are even calling for a boycott of the presidential vote altogether.[26] Indeed, factionalism is what characterized last Friday's *millionyya* – or million-people protest – in Tahrir Square, where dissenting demands dominated the numerous stages that were erected in the square. The inevitable result of these divisions and the alienation of the liberal and secular youth that was behind this promising revolution is a prolonged state of uncertainty marked by chaos and violence.

To avoid these developments from becoming the albatross that will choke the revolution, there is an urgent need for the Egyptian youth to re-take the initiative and mobilize all of their energy and resources to create a single party made out of a coalition of all non-Islamist, non-*old regime* parties to represent the young revolutionaries and their aspirations. Liberal political leaders and intellectuals do recognize the fact that it is the democratic and civil nature of the state (neither theocratic nor military) that distinguishes the revolutionary forces from the rest. Therefore, as much as they have unity of purpose, *they are in dire need of a structurally-sound political unity*.

A glimpse of hope appeared recently with the declaration by Mohamed Elbaradei to establish the *al-Dostour* (Constitution) party to serve as a coalition unifying all civil political groups.[27] If the liberal political leaders do not join such efforts, they risk missing perhaps the last chance to restore the initial objectives of the Egyptian revolution. Secular revolutionary presidential contenders must be governed by, and act on behalf of, the national interests and run as a presidential team (a president and a vice-president) to be supported by the significant voting bloc that the new party could engender.

In preparation for this ambitious political unity, the Egyptian youth should organize itself and mobilize the masses (as they did in the initial stages of the revolution) to take to the streets in the millions in support of a single motto: save the revolution. If the entrenched Mubarak regime could not withstand an 18-day *millionyya* protest, no government or political movement in Egypt, regardless of how powerful they may be, would be able to reject the legitimate demands made by massive, persistent and non-violent protest. To that end the youth movement must insist on the following:

---

25 "I was chosen candidate of Egypt's revolutionary forces: Abul Fotouh," *Al Arabiya*, April 23, 2012, http://www.alarabiya.net/articles/2012/04/23/209789.html.
26 Jano Charbel, "Calls return for boycotting 'murky' elections," *Egypt Independent*, May 19, 2012, http://www.youm7.com/News.asp?NewsID=649223&.
27 "Guide to Egypt's Transition," *Carnegie Endowment for International Peace*, Accessed July 11, 2013, http://egyptelections.carnegieendowment.org/2012/10/31/al-dostour-constitution-party-2.

1. That the constitutional assembly be representative of the entire Egyptian political spectrum, and not dictated by the parliament, even though it is democratically elected (i.e., this should not be the dictatorship of the majority -- to ensure the civil nature of the state).

2. For the elections to be fair, the SCAF and the government should enforce the articles of the current constitutional declaration that forbid the use of religious references in electoral campaigns. Ironically, the MB presidential candidate, Mohamed Morsi, has explicitly stated that he is running under the maxim of: Islam is the Solution.

3. An immediate restructuring and overhaul of the Ministry of the Interior and its intelligence branch, the National Security Service, to ensure their full compliance with human rights while focusing on serious national security threats and not democracy-promotion, NGOs and youth movements as they have in the recent past.

4. Finally, full respect of the transitional period timeline, ending on June 30, 2012, that would ensure the world's confidence in the path Egypt is taking and restore foreign investments.

Some might argue that the youth might not be able to mount such a campaign to resurrect the basic tenants of the revolution and mobilize the public at a time when the average Egyptian is simply exhausted and suffering from a crushing economic crisis, security vacuum, and rampant unemployment (now approaching 25 percent).[28] No one can question this dismal reality and deny these daily hardships, but the revolutionary youth's call to the disgruntled public to awaken to their bitter reality might still resonate as long as: a) they remain truthful to their national inspiration, and b) accept the fact that any revolution will encounter a messy transitional period and will only worsen if nothing is done to stop it.

Unity of purpose, a unified political structure and mobilization of the masses represent the immediate tasks. In the longer term, however, the revolutionary youth's greater challenge is to turn from an elite movement into a grassroots one. This is the lesson that they should learn from their mistake in the 2011 parliamentary elections which were won by the Islamist parties. Although the MB and the Salafists were better financed and better organized, they more importantly *spoke the language of the average Egyptian and understood the importance of working on the priorities of the local communities.* Reaching out to Egypt's poor, which constitute almost 40 percent

---

28 "Egypt's Economic Crisis," *The New York Times,* January 20, 2012. http://www.nytimes.com/2012/01/21/opinion/egypts-economic-crisis.html.

of the population, is the revolutionary youth's major challenge.[29] Most of these young men and women are well-qualified to meet this challenge. Many are already involved in volunteer work that can be re-directed to focus on addressing illiteracy, providing healthcare services and job training, and offering micro-finance – all within a sustainable development and de-centralization model that would certainly secure the revolutionaries a decisive voting bloc in all future elections.

The only loser from the clash between the MB and SCAF is the Egyptian youth and what their revolution stood for. The revolutionary liberal leaders and youth share the responsibility of saving what is left of their revolutionary zeal by closing ranks, running united, and embarking on a massive campaign to protect the democratic, civil nature of the new Egypt by engaging the vast majority of the Egyptian people.

You, the youth of the great nation of Egypt—remember that you do not stand only for your country but for the whole Arab world. What you will do and the zeal with which you carry on the revolutionary process will have a direct impact on every Arab state and the aspiration of more than two hundred million Arab youth who yearn to be free and live with dignity.

Unless you assume this fateful mission and do so now, Egypt will undergo an unending period of chaos and instability, only to be followed by a military dictatorship or theocratic tyranny, and the Arab Spring will have become the cruelest winter of all.

29 "Egypt: Stop forced evictions and consult slum-dwellers to resolve housing crisis," *Amnesty International*, August 23, 2011. http://www.amnesty.org/en/news-and-updates/report/egypt-stop-forced-evictions-and-consult-slum-dwellers-resolve-housing-crisis.

EGYPT'S MUSLIM BROTHERHOOD: PERCEPTION AND REALITY

SEPTEMBER 25, 2012

Those who draw hasty conclusions that an Egypt led by the Muslim Brotherhood (MB) will soon become an Islamic state fashioned after Saudi Arabia or the oppressive regime in Iran neither appreciates Egypt's uniqueness nor its storied history. It is one thing to criticize the MB for their public anti-American and anti-Israeli pronouncements when they were an oppressed group in dire opposition to the Mubarak regime, but it is an altogether different matter now that they rule the country.

For the MB to stay in power and ensure their success when new legislative elections are held, they must adopt a balanced foreign and domestic policy and strive to change the outside world's perception of their hardcore Islamic polity. Mr. Morsi, Egypt's first democratically elected President, knows that he must face reality and focus on economic development, avoid adventurism by preserving the peace with Israel, and maintain good relations with the United States. This political realism still remains consistent with Morsi's professed desire to assert Egypt's role and independence. He insists that while Egypt will not be hostile toward the West and in particular the US, it will not be as compliant as it was under Mubarak's leadership, while restoring Egypt's *sui generis* leadership in the Arab world.

Egypt has a multi-faceted uniqueness that has no parallel among the other Arab states. Egypt has the largest Arab population (nearly 80 million), a cohesive and predominately Sunni population with only one significant minority (Coptic Christians),[30] and stands apart from the tribal-based and/or sectarian societies plagued by sectarian strife like Libya, Syria, Iraq and Bahrain. Moreover, Egypt has a long and continuing history that stretches back nearly 5,000 years, which instills pride in Egyptians and an unmatched historical perspective about themselves as a people. All along, Egypt's political continuity was based on a pharaonic orientation which has centered on strong leadership, particularly on display in the contemporary tenures of Mubarak, Sadat and Nasser. In addition, while the political dynamic has changed in Egypt, there remains a powerful desire to see strong and effective leadership emerge from the revolution as long as it strives toward meeting the premise of revolution- in particular political freedom, human rights and economic development. Lastly, Egypt's traditional leadership role in the Arab world stems from its extraordinarily rich culture cultivated over

---

30 Central Intelligence Agency, "Egypt," *CIA World Factbook*, Updated July 10, 2013, https://www.cia.gov/library/publications/the-world-factbook/geos/eg.html.

thousands of years and its traditional role as leader of the Arab states, a home for the Arab League, and a regular host of Arab summits.[31]

Despite being located at the heart of a tumultuous region, Egypt does not have any external enemies. Gaza represents no threat as Egypt exerts significant influence over Hamas, it does not face any threat from its chaotic southern neighbor, Sudan, and enjoys peace with Israel. Although there are some voices in Egypt who suggest that the peace treaty with Israel should be modified,[32] Egypt's current government remains committed to maintaining the peace treaty that has served its national interests and acted as an anchor for regional stability.[33] Moreover, peace with Israel ensures Washington's continuing economic and military aid and political support, which no Egyptian government, regardless of its political leanings or religious beliefs, can forsake.

In addition, portraying Israel as the culprit behind Egypt's ailments as past governments have done in an effort to distract the public's attention and cover up for its past and present shortcomings will no longer work. Indeed, the MB knows all too well that throughout the revolution, the ire of the people was directed toward the Mubarak regime, not Israel or the United States. The public demanded freedom, adequate social services, and justice that can no longer be drowned out by invoking Israel as the cause of Egypt's malaise. Moreover, though the Egyptian military still remains a powerful institution, it has no reason or motivation to challenge Israel, with whom it has had collaborative relations. On the contrary, President Morsi would like to build on the accord with Israel by finding a solution to the Israeli-Palestinian conflict, which will not only end the conflict but also further enhance Egypt's stature and strengthen regional stability. In a recent interview with *The New York Times*, President Morsi linked the peace treaty with Israel to the US' commitment to Palestinian self-rule.[34] It is that history, traditional role and existing reality that will encourage Egypt's president to pursue a balanced policy in conformity with the unmitigated reality of Egypt.

Although Israel has every reason to suspect the MB's intentions, particularly based on past maligning and criticisms of Israel by MB leaders, it would ultimately be

31 "Egypt hosts summit of new quartet on Syria, hoping to persuade Iran to change stance," *CBS News*, September 11, 2012. http://www.cbsnews.com/8301-202_162-57510283/egypt-hosts-summit-of-new-quartet-on-syria-hoping-to-persuade-iran-to-change-stance/.
32 Maikel Nabil Sanad, "The Egypt-Israel peace treaty is dead," *Haaretz*, September 3, 2012. http://www.haaretz.com/opinion/the-egypt-israel-peace-treaty-is-dead-1.462380?block=true.
33 Adrian Blomfield, "Mohammed Morsi vows to respect Egypt-Israel peace treaty," *The Telegraph*, August 28, 2012. http://www.telegraph.co.uk/news/worldnews/africaandindianocean/egypt/9504601/Mohammed-Morsi-vows-to-respect-Egypt-Israel-peace-treaty.html.
34 David D. Kirkpatrick and Steven Erlanger, "Egypt's New Leader Spells Out Terms for U.S.-Arab Ties," *The New York Times*, September 22, 2012, http://www.nytimes.com/2012/09/23/world/middleeast/egyptian-leader-mohamed-morsi-spells-out-terms-for-us-arab-ties.html?pagewanted=all.

prudent of Israel to change its perception of and approach toward the MB. Israel must face reality and employ the policy of "respect and suspect" by giving the MB the opportunity to prove itself. While Morsi and the MB are attempting to place Egypt on a new path, their rise to power makes it imperative as stated to face reality as well: Israel is not a reality they can wish away. While the ongoing turmoil in the Middle East and Arab upheavals may take decades to settle, the Israeli-Palestinian conflict cannot be wished away and neither Egypt nor Israel can wait it out. Thus, both countries under the MB's leadership have a historic opportunity to work together to bring an end to the conflict.

Notwithstanding the relationship between Hamas and Iran, or the collapsed ties between Hamas and Syria, Hamas, more than any time before, depends on the MB, of which it is an offshoot, for political and strategic support. Recent unrest in the Sinai has provided the MB with an opportunity to rein Hamas in to a more moderate position toward Israel and avoid any provocation.[35] Indeed, the MB, as I was told by a high Egyptian official, does not wish to choose between aiding Hamas against Israel or leaving Hamas to Israel's whims in case of a violent conflict between the two sides. Either situation will place the MB in an extremely difficult bind.

For this reason, the MB advised Hamas to keep a low profile and to moderate its position toward Israel, and exerted pressure on Hamas to forsake violence as a tool by which to achieve its political objectives of destroying Israel and establishing a Palestinian state in its stead. The MB, however, will be eager to play a more active and direct role, especially if Israel makes some goodwill gestures toward the Palestinians such as the release of prisoners, easing the blockade on Gaza, and declaring a temporary halt on the settlements' expansion, while crediting the MB as the player behind such Israeli moves.

Although the Egyptian government under Morsi's leadership certainly hopes to carve an independent path in order to project itself as a renewed regional leader and not merely a conduit for US or Western interests, Morsi also knows that Egypt's economic, political, and military well-being depends on the US' continued direct and indirect support. To demonstrate his independence, however, and to the chagrin of the US, Morsi decided to attend the Non-Aligned Movement Summit in Tehran. While there, however, Morsi used his appearance at the summit to publicly lambaste Syria as an "oppressive regime,"[36] which amounts to an indictment of Iran's cynical support for the Assad regime. Morsi's decision to make his first

35 "Sinai Crisis Gives Israel, Egypt and Hamas a Common Enemy," *Bloomberg*, August 13, 2012. http://www.bloomberg.com/news/2012-08-13/sinai-crisis-gives-israel-egypt-and-hamas-a-common-enemy.html.
36 Ramin Mostaghim, "Egypt's Morsi denounces Syria as 'oppressive regime' at Iran summit," *Los Angeles Times*, August 30, 2012. http://latimesblogs.latimes.com/world_now/2012/08/egypt-morsi-denounces-syria-iran-summit.html.

international trip as president to Saudi Arabia[37] should further allay some concerns about the MB government as it gives another indication that Morsi and the MB are more likely to join the Arab moderate camp that seeks a comprehensive peace with Israel based on the Arab Peace Initiative.

The revolution in Egypt has instilled a definite sense of freedom on the part of the public, who, even after the fall of Mubarak, filled Tahrir Square demanding economic development, better education, improved health care, and the chance to live a meaningful life with dignity. The day-to-day dissatisfaction in Egypt, however, remains endemic as the economy continues to be plagued by gross inefficiencies that further aggravate mass poverty and high unemployment.[38]

Since Egypt still relies on global financial sources such as the International Monetary Fund (IMF) and the World Bank (WB) in addition to loans from Saudi Arabia and the United States,[39] it is virtually impossible for the MB to take any course of action that dramatically deviates from Western "prescriptions" or goes against the spirit of Egypt's revolution. Now that the public has the courage and knows effective methods of taking to the streets and protesting, it will be able to topple any government that fails to deliver on its promises.

The unparalleled story of Egypt was on stark display throughout the course of its revolution, which was the shortest in length, relatively less violent, and caused the powerful military apparatus to be upended and sidetracked. The MB knows that Egypt's future and its leadership role will ultimately *be determined by meeting its domestic needs* and the desire to remain an anchor of regional peace. Thus, maintaining good relations with both the West and the wider Arab/Muslim world while seeking an Israeli-Palestinian peace to further Morsi's domestic agenda will become central to the success of the MB's governance.

37 "Egypt's President Morsi to visit Saudi Arabia on Wednesday," *Ahram Online*, July 10, 2012. http://english.ahram.org.eg/News/47362.aspx.

38 Scott Sayare, "A Dictator Is Gone, but Egypt's Traffic and Congestion Seem Immovable," *The New York Times*, September 10, 2012. http://www.nytimes.com/2012/09/11/world/middleeast/for-egyptians-no-relief-from-cairos-infamous-traffic.html.

39 "Egypt Hopes for Loan as IMF Revives Talks," *The Wall Street Journal*, August 22, 2012. http://online.wsj.com/article/SB10000872396390444358404577605420315385632.html.

YEMEN

YEMEN

SAVING YEMEN FROM ITSELF

SEPTEMBER 10, 2012

Yemen as a nation has gone through a dramatic turmoil brought about by internal violent conflicts occurring over the last several decades. The forced resignation of President Ali Abdullah Saleh (replaced by Vice President Abd Rabbuh Mansour Hadi) in February, along with the formation of a transitional unity government, has had little effect on the fundamental issues bearing down on Yemen.[1] Although recent efforts made by the Saudi government to raise billions of dollars geared toward the development of Yemen[2] is a welcome sign, there is little assurance that these funds will in fact stabilize the situation and save the country from itself unless the money is delivered and invested wisely.

Yemen's internal conditions are and have been dismal for decades, with nearly seven million citizens deprived of basic necessities, a half million children affected by acute malnutrition,[3] and a startling 50 percent unemployment rate.[4] The media in and outside of Yemen have scarcely reported on this dire situation, choosing instead to focus on major violent incidents committed by al-Qaeda and other extremist militia in the Arabian Peninsula (yet only to the extent that they affected neighboring Arab countries or the United States). Moreover, despite the political changes, it has and continues to be extremely difficult to assess what is really taking place on the ground, and the situation remains murky at best.

---

1 Faisal Darem, "Yemen forms national reconciliation government," *Al-Shorfa*, December 8, 2011. http://al-shorfa.com/en_GB/articles/meii/features/main/2011/12/08/feature-02.
2 "Global donors pledge $6.4bn to stabilise fragile Yemen," *BBC News*, September 5, 2012. http://www.bbc.co.uk/news/world-middle-east-19490498.
3 "Yemen 2012 Humanitarian Response Plan," *UNICEF*, accessed September 1, 2012. https://docs.unocha.org/sites/dms/CAP/2012_Yemen_HRP.pdf.
4 "Yemen says Saudi Arabia to donate $1 billion to support currency," *Reuters*, August 29, 2012. http://www.reuters.com/article/2012/08/29/us-yemen-aid-idUSBRE87S14Q20120829.

While the law establishing the transitional government was lofty in content, it has had little effect on the day-to-day life of ordinary Yemenites.[5]

The lamentable lack of attention to Yemen was also precipitated by the country's marginal political influence both regionally and certainly within the international arena. Although in the latest meetings in Riyadh international donors pledged nearly $6.5 billion for Yemen's development and security, these funds may still meet the fate of earlier monetary pledges made this past May, much of which was either not delivered or was largely misappropriated with little effect on changing the quo.[6] Successive governments in Yemen under the deposed President Saleh's 33-year reign were plagued by rampant corruption and patronage which continue unabated to this day, particularly since many of the corrupt officials continue to hold the same positions they held in the previous government.

Assuming that much of the money pledged in May (and more recently) is finding its way to the Yemeni treasury, the paramount concern remains how best to utilize these funds in order to prevent Yemen from becoming a failed state, if it has not already. To begin with, some of these funds must go toward improving the security conditions throughout the country. As long as al-Qaeda and other militant Islamist groups continue to violently undermine and sabotage any efforts to rebuild Yemen as a state, developing a lasting peace will remain on the wishful list. For the security forces to become effective, money in and of itself will not suffice to improve the overall security vacuum. External advisers and trainers from some regional states and forces such as Saudi Arabia, Egypt, Turkey, and the US should devote time, energy, and resources to train Yemen's internal security forces, improve intelligence, and provide these forces with proper military hardware to deal with the insurgency and systematically disrupt and eventually prevent al-Qaeda from operating almost freely throughout the Arabian Peninsula.

Moreover, a significant portion of these funds should be channeled toward the development of crucial infrastructure such as roads, schools and medical clinics. Although these projects should be undertaken by the government, they must nevertheless be supervised by representatives of the donor countries. These states, specifically Saudi Arabia, ought to ensure that these funds are not squandered by corrupt officials and however critical the internal security may be, the development of the infrastructure cannot wait until all security requirements are fully met. To have the most effect, the funds should be divided into installments. Before providing the second installment,

5 "Law on Transitional Justice and National Reconciliation," *The Peace and Justice Initiative,* accessed September 2, 2012. http://www.peaceandjusticeinitiative.org/wp-content/uploads/2012/03/Yemeni-draft-Transitional-Justice-Law.pdf.
6 "'Friends of Yemen' Pledge $4 Billion in Aid," *Voice of America,* May 23, 2012. http://www.voanews.com/content/friends_of_yemen_pledge_4_billion_in_aid/940066.html.

Yemeni authorities must demonstrate that the initial payment has been utilized for what was intended by providing accountability and transparency.

In addition to security and infrastructure, sustainable participatory development projects should receive special attention. Although building infrastructure and institutions necessary to create jobs and improve the overall quality of life remains the purview of the government, empowering ordinary citizens through sustainable development should attain top priority. Sustainable economic development invariably creates wealth both for the communities that adopt such projects and for the state treasury, which can generate more income through increased tax revenues. In turn, these funds (taxes) can be used toward improving the social safety net and the overall health of the economy. The great benefit in engaging in sustainable development is that small communities are empowered to collectively decide through advice and consent on projects of their choice, from which they can benefit while the principles of democratic culture are simultaneously fostered. It is worthy to note that such projects require limited capital and do not necessitate an infusion of new capital and advanced technology. In fact, ten percent of the money pledged ($650 million) could provide more than one million Yemenites a decent living and restore their basic human rights while fostering democratic principles.

It must be noted that none of the three objectives should take preference over the others; improving security, building new infrastructure and implementing sustainable development projects all need to be tackled concurrently. In the interim, an emergency supply of food, medical aid and other necessary provisions must be rushed to despondent families to save the lives of nearly one million who are on the verge of dying from malnutrition, particularly women and children.

Saudi Arabia is an extremely important player in regards to what is happening in Yemen. First, many of the terrorist activities that have occurred in Saudi Arabia were traced to Yemeni citizens largely instigated by al-Qaeda. Secondly, due to Saudi Arabia's proximity to Yemen, particularly their shared eastern border where a large Shiite concentration and many oil deposits are located,[7] Saudi Arabia has every interest in ensuring Yemen's stability, which informs their substantial contributions of three billion dollars at the so-called "Friends of Yemen" meetings in Riyadh. Third, should Yemen become a failed state, Saudi Arabia will be directly affected by the threats of mass refugees and a terrorist infiltration that will permeate the entire Gulf region.

7 "Yemen," *European Institute for Research on Mediterranean and Euro-Arab Cooperation*, Accessed July 12, 2013, http://www.medea.be/en/countries/yemen/yemen/; see also, Mark Dennis, "Yemeni-Saudi Border Dispute Flares Over Oil Discoveries," *Christian Science Monitor*, May 21, 1992, http://www.csmonitor.com/1992/0521/21052.html

The current reconciliation government must ensure that it is representative of all segments of Yemeni society and in particular must seek, with the support of Saudi Arabia and neighboring countries, a dialogue with the Houthi movement which controls significant portions of northern Yemen.[8] Although the conflict between this tribe and the central government goes back many decades, it is nearly impossible to stabilize Yemen without finding a peaceful settlement with the secessionist groups who have established their own autonomous zone.

By providing funds, however important and critical they may be to addressing Yemen's malaise, the efforts to save the country must remain an Arab enterprise. That said, only the Yemeni people, with the helping hand of the international community, can pull the country back from the brink of an increasingly imminent disaster.

8 Madeleine Wells, "Yemen's Houthi movement and the revolution," *Foreign Policy*, February 27, 2012. http://mideast.foreignpolicy.com/posts/2012/02/27/yemen_s_houthi_movement_and_the_revolution.

LIBYA

QADDAFI: SURVIVAL IS NOT AN OPTION

PRESIDENT OBAMA HAS ALREADY DEVELOPED A REPUTATION FOR TOUGH TALK AND LITTLE ACTION. WORSE YET, THE UNITED STATES' CAUTIOUSNESS IN THE WAKE OF THE LESSONS OF IRAQ AND AFGHANISTAN—WHILE UNDERSTANDABLE—THREATEN TO PAINT A PICTURE OF THE OBAMA WHITE HOUSE AS WEAK, INEFFECTUAL AND COWARDLY.

MARCH 22ND, 2011

Just days into a military campaign to cripple Colonel Muammar al-Qaddafi's ability to launch attacks against the rebel stronghold of Benghazi, the effort is threatened by obfuscation and lack of leadership. The same kind of foot-dragging deliberations which escalated the situation by enabling time for Qaddafi's forces to turn the tide against the early advances of the rebels, now threaten to leave Libya in an open-ended civil war. By allowing such a dire situation to fester, the United States is abdicating its responsibility to provide moral leadership.

Instead, the U.S. should be neither apologetic nor abashed in clearly stating its interests: a removal of Muammar al-Qaddafi from his fiefdom in favor of a stable path toward an Arab and Libyan-led reconstitution of the Libyan state that gives voice to all the people of Libya, rather than to a single madman in Tripoli. The early impotence of the international community to respond to the tragic bloodshed was shameful. But a precedent has been set in all Arab capitals, including Tripoli: if the people demand and are willing to die for it, you must go. The success of the Arab revolutions of 2011, the fate of the Libyan people and security across North Africa and Europe demand that Qaddafi be removed from power—*his survival is not an option*.

The hesitance of the United States to intervene—and "nation-build"—in another Middle Eastern nation is understandable. Engagement in Afghanistan was justified but is now languishing, and the American intervention in Iraq was both ill-advised and poorly executed. But the United States need not apologize for extending moral leadership when it is direly needed, or for pursuing distinct American interests.

President Obama should first and foremost be preoccupied with these factors, not with fear that any form of intervention should be avoided due to the learned mistakes made in Iraq and Afghanistan. We also should not fear questions as to our regional positions. Our policy to support the leadership in Bahrain is based clearly on our interest to safeguard the Gulf from Iran's influence and threats, and to protect our strategic military bases. This is no secret, and we shouldn't hesitate to be clear and even bold about expressing our strategic interests, especially when they are consistent with the national interests of our Arab allies in the region. This should not preclude our continuing efforts to promote political reforms in Bahrain.

Libya, however, is indeed different than Bahrain. Despite claims by analysts that Qaddafi is of minimal concern to the United States' national security, his reign presents a different challenge to the White House. If the United States were to allow such a lunatic to hold onto power and slaughter his own people, any notion of the United States playing a stabilizing and positive role in the Middle East will be finished. Even so, speaking with the media on Sunday, March 20, Admiral Mike Mullen, the Chairman of the Joint Chiefs of Staff, stated that "The focus of the United Nations Security Council resolution was really Benghazi specifically, and to protect civilians, and we've done that – we have started to do that… This is not about going after Qaddafi himself or attacking him at this particular point in time."[1] Vice Admiral Bill Gortney, a Pentagon Spokesman, was much more direct when he recently told reporters, "We are not going after Qaddafi."[2]

The murky goals of Operation Odyssey Dawn are already being criticized in capitals across the globe. It is simply unrealistic to suggest that an international coalition can provide sufficient support for the Libyan opposition merely by providing defense from the air alone. Furthermore, if the White House continues to display an opaque and reluctant U.S. role, it will only serve to solidify a dangerous status quo: a fractured Libya in which an enraged Qaddafi continues the bloodshed against an ill-equipped opposition whom the international coalition refuses to meaningfully support. Doing so will perpetuate the ever-strengthening view that President Obama is a weak, even cowardly, leader who has refused to stand up for America's principles and interests because of his reluctance to use military force at a time when U.S. forces are greatly extended. However, there is an alternative for President Obama to pursue: providing leadership for a coalition of Western and Arab nations to remove Qaddafi from power (which most Arab states would welcome) and map out a transition toward a proper system of governance unique

1 Mike Mullen, interview by Chris Wallace, *Fox News*, March 20, 2011. http://www.jcs.mil/speech.aspx?id=1550.
2 Mark Thompson, "Gaddafi Not Even a Target, Never Mind a Bullseye," *Time*, March 20, 2011. http://nation.time.com/2011/03/20/gaddafi-not-even-a-target-never-mind-a-bullseye/.

to the tribal traditions of Libyan society. It is not the easy thing to do, nor perhaps the most popular, but it is the right thing to do, for the people of Libya and for U.S. interests. We should get started right now.

The Arab League's courageous support for the no-fly zone was a central part of the rationale for the current military actions underway. The Arab League should continue to acknowledge the change and reform taking shape across the Arab world by contributing to a campaign to oust Qaddafi from power in favor of a government that would serve the interests of the Libyan people. The United States and its Western allies need to be frank with the Arab world in both *public and private.* If you prefer Western intervention to be limited, you must step up and provide military support of your own, which would receive the full support and guidance of the United States, Britain and France, among others.

The United States could start by pressing for a two-part strategy. First is clarifying the goals of the international coalition's current campaign, unabashedly. This campaign is indeed about the much-feared catch phrase of the moment: "regime change." However, unlike Iraq, this effort will be one that serves to support the Libyan people in finishing a job that they started. This first phase should include clear communications to the Libyan military and officer corps that abandoning Qaddafi now will be the only alternative to being killed or arrested and tried for war crimes. This will encourage further defection, especially of the high-ranking officers. Second, an Arab-led coalition should provide military support to oust Qaddafi, and then work alongside a reconstituted Libyan military to combine the various Libyan tribes—whose internal rivalry has been substantially mitigated in recent decades—into a national council. Such a council could then serve to navigate the country through a stable transition toward a system of government that suits the still uniquely tribal character of the country.

An Arab-led coalition could be composed of a variety of Arab nations, including Qatar, who is already contributing to the current campaign. Chief among the coalition, however, should be Libya's reforming North African neighbors, specifically Egypt, Tunisia, and Morocco. Providing leading support would re-establish Egypt's leadership in the Arab world and safeguard the stability of its neighborhood. The symbolism of Tunisia's aid would link the Libyan campaign to revolutionary protests throughout the region, which were sparked when Tunisian street vendor Mohammed Bouazizi set himself on fire and have lasted through the Libyan rebels' courageous stand against Qaddafi. Morocco's participation would be based on the reforms it has set in motion, and would signal that the longstanding rulers of the region are indeed prepared to engage in activities that provide a greater voice to their people. The Arab street is fully supportive of removing Qaddafi, and for his neighboring nations, the more-deranged-than-ever Qaddafi continuing at the helm in Libya could significantly jeopardize the hope generated by their recent reforms. Rather than serve as the next domino in the wave of Arab revolutions in 2011, Qaddafi's hold on power could lead to an even more radical regime in Libya, which has been known to pursue weapons of mass destruction, and will now have the pretext to seek revenge against huge swaths of its own population.

In short, the threat of a lunatic Qaddafi with a vendetta against his own people and the world is one that the global community, and in particular Qaddafi's neighbors, cannot afford to test. That is why such a coalition to oust him should garner the support of both the United Nations and the Arab League. It should have a limited mandate to provide stability for the establishment of a new Libyan government. Ousting Qaddafi is the right thing to do; it should not be an insurmountable task. Otherwise, if an emboldened Qaddafi were to stay in power, the United States' interests would also undoubtedly be threatened. Even more, the credibility and moral leadership of the White House would be completely shattered. To be sure, the United States must be systematic, intelligent, and efficient with how it chooses to respond, but it must be clear about its goals. Despite Qaddafi's threatening warnings of a long war, his military infrastructure is poor and his Soviet-era weaponry considerably antiquated. With airstrikes already limiting Qaddafi's capacity, the focus should now be shifted to ousting him from power, and "day after" planning should commence immediately. In fact, once Qaddafi realizes that the international community is determined to oust him from power by whatever means necessary, he will seek to negotiate a peaceful exit.

The notion that a military campaign could leave Qaddafi in place must be completely discredited. If the youth in Libya, who have so courageously stood up against the much more powerful and ruthless Libyan dictator, fail to oust him because of such Western cowardice, it will serve as a stain on this White House and a cancer on the hope and optimism that the Arab revolutions of 2011 have generated.

ELECTIONS IN LIBYA SHOULD BE DEFERRED

THE TRANSITIONAL GOVERNMENT MUST FIRST FOCUS ON INTERNAL SECURITY, RECONCILIATION, AND ECONOMIC DEVELOPMENT TO PROVIDE A STRONG FOUNDATION FOR FREE NATIONAL ELECTIONS AND A STABLE NEW POLITICAL ORDER

AUGUST 28, 2011

While the Libyan rebels have rightfully celebrated the ousting of Muammar al-Qaddafi after his 42-year reign in Libya, turning him from all-powerful dictator to a cowered fugitive, the real challenges for a new Libya are just beginning. The road to writing a new constitution, forging new political parties, rebuilding a battered infrastructure, developing a broken economy, and fostering civil society will be long, difficult, and punctuated by violence. Having starved his people of any semblance of participatory governance, Libyans must begin to pick up the pieces Qaddafi left behind in order to build a foundation for a free, secure, and stable nation.

Restoring law and order throughout the country must be the first priority. As long as Qaddafi loyalists maintain pockets of resistance (and Qaddafi himself remains a fugitive), Libya's transition cannot begin in earnest. Second, Qaddafi must be captured and full control of the country must be won before security and basic public services such as electricity and clean, running water can be fully and reliably restored.

Collecting weapons will be a key task in this effort, including the large arsenal looted by rebels from Qaddafi's Tripoli compound. Reinstating police forces and ensuring that they are fully paid and functioning properly to maintain internal security is *sine qua non* to achieving any additional progress.

Many Libyans have suffered under the ruthlessness of Qaddafi's internal security forces. Revenge and retribution will only be a natural course of action for many Libyans to settle old grievances. The transitional government should learn from the mistakes made in Iraq and begin immediately a campaign of reconciliation by welcoming the integration of police and soldiers who had been loyal to Qaddafi, rather than disbanding them and fueling further violent retributions which would derail efforts to establish genuine security in the country.

Healing rather than exacerbating the historic east/west divide in the country must begin now. Consolidating factions to form a government that "affirms the Islamic identity of the Libyan People, its commitment to the moderate Islamic values, its full

73

rejection to the extremist ideas and its commitment to combating them in all circumstances," as stated by the NTC in a March 30th statement, would be a critical step toward a stable and prosperous Libya.[3]

If a thriving economy is to be built and the hordes of foreign expatriates are to return to Libya, establishing security throughout the country will be crucial. As security comes into place, the NTC, the legal authority in Libya recognized by scores of countries and the Arab League, must work to bring the nation's oil production back online in order to infuse the country with much-needed capital. Industry analysts speculate that it could take as many as two years to bring production to the level produced during Qaddafi's reign, which amount to 1.6 million barrels a day. In fact, as the head of the Libyan Stabilization Team in the NTC, Ahmed Jehani, recently told the BBC, the "utter neglect" of the oil industry and national infrastructure under Qaddafi could take as much as a decade to rehabilitate.[4]

At only 60,000 barrels a day today, the unrest in the country has left the NTC with a considerable task in overhauling the state's handling of oil contracts to ensure both transparency and equitable distribution of oil wealth throughout Libya. Finally, since oil production accounts for as much as 95 percent of Libya's export earnings, and resumption of full oil production will take time,[5] the gradual unfreezing of Qaddafi's assets, estimated at over $100 billion,[6] is critical to meet the financial obligation of the government to remain solvent and retain the people's confidence.

Genuine economic development will be central for a country that experienced over 30 percent unemployment prior to the outbreak of the uprising.[7] Yet there are opportunities for growth should the NTC prove successful in maintaining the kind of competent governance that can generate confidence for companies and investors. Libya could capitalize on its coastal location and proximity to Europe by investing in robust tourism, industry and manufacturing. In addition, the building of educational institutions to provide young Libyans the opportunity to acquire necessary modern skills to develop and build these industries will open the door to greater foreign investments, and with that, an expanded job market.

3 "Statement of the Transitional National Council on Counter-Terrorism," *The Libyan Interim National Council*, March 30, 2011. http://www.ntclibya.org/english/counter-terrorism/.
4 "Libya crisis: a decade to rebuild Libya, says NTC," *BBC News*, August 26, 2011. http://www.bbc.co.uk/news/business-14675948.
5 Richard Anderson, "Libya oil: The race to turn the taps back on," *BBC News*, September 8, 2011, http://www.bbc.co.uk/news/business-14806100.
6 Paul Richter, "Estimate of Gaddafi's hidden assets 'staggering'," *The Washington Post*, October 21, 2011, http://articles.washingtonpost.com/2011-10-21/world/35279668_1_moammar-gaddafi-libyan-citizen-libyan-authorities.
7 "Libya," *CIA World Factbook*, Updated July 10, 2013, https://www.cia.gov/library/publications/the-world-factbook/geos/ly.html.

Restoring internal security, reconciling between the old and the new guard, and making a major effort in rebuilding the economy will lay the strong foundation needed to move toward significant democratic reforms. The transition to a new central and democratic government will be long and arduous. Qaddafi left Libya with nothing: no political parties, no civil society, no non-governmental organizations, and no parliament.

The political transformation should begin by developing a new Libyan National Assembly representing all corners of the country. Although much has been done to prepare for the writing of a new constitution, the formal committee that will be officially tasked to write a new constitution should be selected from and empowered by the Libyan National Assembly. A successful Libyan constitutional framework is one that will reflect the needs of the people and allow tribal leaders to have a say as long as human rights remain constitutionally enshrined and fully enforced.

The planned general elections must be postponed for at least two years. Indeed, elections in the near term, as the US and EU countries are prone to push for, would be a catastrophic mistake for Libya. In Tunisia and Egypt, observers have witnessed the growing pains of the nascent democratic movements in nations where dictators were ousted, but the civil society infrastructures in those countries are far superior to the shambles that Qaddafi left behind.

Political parties must be given time and resources to organize, develop political platforms, and familiarize the public with their stand on various issues affecting the country's future security and economic developments. Opting for elections too soon would give too much credence and undue power to isolated tribal factions and Islamists, especially the Libyan Islamic Fighting Group (LIFG), which is the only group likely to be able to garner loyalty in the immature Libyan political landscape. It remains to be seen if, in a new Libya, the remnants of the LIFG will adhere to their November 2009 pledge to renounce jihadist violence against "women, children, elderly people, priests, messengers, traders and the like."[8]

The West was right to utilize NATO to assist the rebels in overthrowing the lunatic that ruled Libya for 42 years. The strategy was successful chiefly because while the West aided the rebels' fight, the victory was led, and ultimately achieved, by Libyans themselves. The construction of a new Libya must also be achieved in the same manner. While the international community has a critical role to play in infusing the country with much-needed investment, the success of the Libyan transition will ultimately hinge on continued determination by the Libyan people themselves.

---

8 Nic Robertson and Paul Cruickshank, "New jihad code threatens al Qaeda," *CNN*, November 10, 2009. http://edition.cnn.com/2009/WORLD/africa/11/09/libya.jihadi.code/.

Demonstrating progress by the NTC and communicating the steps toward a strong and secure Libya while *adhering to human rights from day one* will be critical to engender confidence among all Libyans. While permanent change may be slow to achieve, progressive change will begin at once.

SYRIA

SYRIA

A WILD AND FAR-FETCHED IDEA

WILL ASSAD HAVE THE COURAGE AND THE VISION TO RISE TO THE HISTORIC OCCASION AND CHANGE THE GEOPOLITICAL DYNAMICS THROUGHOUT THE MIDDLE EAST?

APRIL 18, 2011

Time and circumstances have presented Syria's President Bashar Al-Assad with a clear choice: Continue to convey an image of an impotent dictator sounding eerily similar to the embattled, aging, and ousted despots who have failed to meet their people's needs, blaming foreign conspiracies for their shortcomings, or display bold leadership and vision in order to use the opportunity of the unrest to institute basic reforms and turn toward the West. The notion that Assad would do the latter is perhaps wild and far-fetched, but the benefits Syria would reap and the effect on other countries involved as a result would be of a magnitude that could change the geopolitical landscape of the Middle East in an unprecedented way.

Assad's March 30th address was disappointing. Prior to the speech, there had been great anticipation that he would remove the emergency law that has been in place since 1963,[1] as well as institute other reforms to gradually open Syrian society in ways that would strengthen Syria's domestic and foreign policies. Instead, Assad provided a scapegoat for Syria's problems: a conspiracy led chiefly by Israel and the United States to undermine Syrian "stability." Of course, there is no foreign conspiracy, and Assad knows it, and if he continues to ignore the wave of protests that have arrived at his doorstep, he will do so at his own peril. Certainly Syria's people do not buy Assad's tall tale.

Syria is known among the Arab states for the quality and quantity of its intellectuals and academics. Syria's youth are increasingly demanding greater freedoms and access to the world. For these intellectuals and young men and women, Assad's *j' accuse* speech must have rightfully appeared as outdated and hackneyed rhetoric. The Syrian people also know that in the current context, Assad's ability to employ

---

1 "Syria: decision already made to lift emergency law," *Al Arabiya*, March 27, 2011, http://www.alarabiya.net/articles/2011/03/27/143167.html.

79

ruthlessness to maintain his regime is limited. The days of Hama, when Hafez Assad reportedly killed thousands in leveling part of the city to clamp down on the Muslim Brotherhood in 1982, are over. The more Syrians killed by Assad's regime, the more likely that the Syrian people and the international community will resort to greater and more lethal methods to bring about his downfall.

The choice for Assad, however, is not between continuing his iron-fist reign and undertaking political reforms. Some argue that lifting the emergency law, which he promised to do in his speech last Saturday, will undermine the regime. I don't buy it. There are plenty of steps Assad can take to promote the kind of *gradual* reforms that would address the basic demands of his people while maintaining the stability and fabric of his regime. However, to do so successfully, he must begin to reassess his relations with Iran and its surrogates Hamas and Hezbollah. Assad's alliance with these entities has proved successful in recent years. He has captured the attention of the region—and the United States—while overcoming the suspicion and scrutiny of the investigation into the assassination of former Lebanese Prime Minister Rafik Hariri, and has used Syria's ties to Iran and extremist groups to gain leverage over potential future talks with the U.S. and Israel.

But now the tide has turned in the region, and to rely on this alliance would be to bet on the wrong horse. Iran is embattled with its own domestic unrest, and when push comes to shove, neither Israel nor the US will allow Iran to become a regional hegemon equipped with a nuclear weapon. Meanwhile, Hezbollah's allegiance to Iran and increasing influence in Lebanon will soon grow beyond Syria's control. Even Hamas seeks a prolonged cease-fire with Israel[2] and is in unity talks with Fatah as the Palestinians look to the United Nations General Assembly for recognition of their own state come September. Neither of these groups have the appetite to seriously challenge Israel and face the prospect of utter destruction. Moreover, Syria must now deal with its own internal combustion and, in this regional context, Assad's current positioning offers him little hope for a successful, viable strategy (which may have prompted his second speech).

Assad should take heed of the events in Tunisia and Egypt and the uprisings that are sweeping the entire Arab world. Perhaps more than any other Arab leader, however, he might be able to weather the storm of discontent, provided he resolves to adopt a strikingly new strategy. Why can he survive where others could not? He is young, Western-oriented and educated, has access to vast intellectual resources in his country,

---

2 Amos Harel, "Hamas has requested a cease fire, Israel officials say," *Haaretz*, April 9, 2011, http://www.haaretz.com/news/diplomacy-defense/hamas-has-requested-a-cease-fire-israel-officials-say-1.354971.

and—most importantly—he is in a pivotal position in the Middle East. This last point is particularly compelling for the United States. Rather than fight against the wind of revolutionary change, Assad should go with it. In doing so, he should follow the footsteps of Egyptian President Anwar el-Sadat. Sadat's abandonment of the Soviet Union in favor of the United States was a bold and far-sighted move. If Assad were to take a similar step in connection with Iran, he could reap the benefits of the return of the Golan Heights from Israel, a strengthened economy, and a more influential position of stability and leadership at the nexus of the Arab world. He doesn't have to completely sever ties with Iran and unsavory extremist groups in a flash.

The moment Assad turns to the United States, he will be sending a positive signal to Israel, albeit tacitly, and could begin some basic reforms of the U.S.-Syria relationship. This will translate to diminishing ties with Iran as well as reduced logistical and financial support for Hamas and Hezbollah. Assad can turn to the West without overtly declaring his intention to withdraw from the Iranian orbit, but in effect still withdraw. Furthermore, he does not need to forsake Hamas and Hezbollah. Syria's continued relationship with them could place it in an even more significant role through which to influence these groups to abandon their self-destructive dream of destroying Israel and instead join to advance regional peace and security.

Despite the Syrian crackdown and killings of protestors, the United States hasn't recalled its newly installed ambassador for consultation. While the White House is still trying to undermine Iranian President Mahmoud Ahmadinejad, it recognizes the potential Bashar al-Assad has to fundamentally change the geopolitical dynamic, if he makes the right moves. The United States should now begin to tacitly convey that he should make gradual reforms, making good on his promise to remove the emergency law and expand economic and press freedoms. In addition, if Assad begins to look west, the U.S. must have the will, and program in place, to support him. Throughout the Middle East, the United States has shown that if its national security interests and the interests of its allies (Bahrain and Saudi Arabia as a case in point) demand that a leader plays a critical role—like Syria could—in promoting those interests, they will work with this leader. A byproduct of this process would be to bolster the stability and position of Syria in the region.

The United States' goals in its engagement with Syria are well-known: to weaken Iran and its proxies Hamas and Hezbollah. For Assad to advance these goals, he will need something substantial in return. Contrary to the beliefs of many, the U.S. has a great deal to offer: A new economic relationship and U.S. aid (along the lines of that provided to Egypt following the Egypt-Israel peace treaty) as well as a return of the Golan Heights upon successful, U.S.-facilitated and incentivized negotiations between Syria and Israel, while carefully addressing the latter's national security concerns.

What kind of legacy does Assad want to leave behind? The young 45-year-old Syrian leader has a historic opportunity to oversee, and even lead, the Arab world through a period of major transformation. However, to do so he must stop acting like the old dictators in the region, and act more like the kind of strong, forward-looking leader the protestors on the streets demand. Furthermore, he must stop the violent confrontations on the streets which will greatly advance the prospect of his ouster, and the subsequent uncertainty that would replace him. Assad may be able to create a model of change without relinquishing power as long as he does it sooner rather than later. Otherwise, Assad will increasingly be on the defensive and lose tremendous ground as time elapses. Yes, he is surrounded by an entrenched *ancien régime* that has vested interests in maintaining the status quo, but they too know that the current situation is no longer sustainable and their days in power are numbered unless there is change, for which the public yearns.

Assad already knows what chips the United States is willing to play. It is in this administration's interest to validate the engagement policy it has pursued with Syria, by bringing Assad to moderation and to the Western camp, particularly as President Obama faces myriad challenges in the region and an upcoming presidential re-election campaign. The question now is: what chips will Assad be willing to play, and can he rise to the occasion? Perhaps not. If he does, however, he must decide quickly, or he may soon find that he has no chips left at all.

IT IS TOO LATE FOR ASSAD

JUNE 24, 2011

One month after the uprisings began in Syria, I wrote that President Bashar al-Assad had a choice: "Continue to convey an image of an inept dictator … or display bold leadership and vision in order to use the opportunity of the unrest to institute basic reforms…"[3] In his May 19th remarks on the Middle East, President Obama posited a similar choice for the Syria regime, stating: "President Assad now has a choice: He can lead that transition [to democracy], or get out of the way."[4] In a speech to his nation last Monday, President Assad once again missed the opportunity to face reality and address the real grievances of his people. Although he acknowledged that there are some peaceful protesters with legitimate concerns, he once again blamed much of the unrest and violence on "vandals," "outlaws," and "radical and blasphemous intellectuals."[5]

Most observers dismissed Assad's speech as being too broad with no specifics about reforms, giving the protesters no hope for substantive change for the better in the immediate future. Since his speech, instead of showing restraint and beginning an honest national dialogue, Assad continues to use brutal force to subdue the protesters, losing what's left of his credibility. It has become clear that Assad has made his choice. With over 1,400 Syrians killed, more than 10,000 fleeing the country, and as many languishing in jail, it is too late for Assad to redeem himself. And yet the international community remains feeble, doing nothing about it. Without meaningful action, Assad is likely to seek dangerous and desperate measures to maintain power, and Syria could become engulfed in the kind of prolonged, internecine sectarian violence that serves as a gaping pattern of instability affecting the entire region.

The beginning of the end for Assad may be found in the northern city of Jisr Al-Shugour. There, Assad's regime claimed that 120 Syrian soldiers were killed by violent demonstrators. However, widespread reports from thousands of Syrians who fled the city to nearby Turkey tell a different tale: that the officers were killed after deserting the military and fighting their former comrades-in-arms. The Assad regime's response, which was to essentially level half the city in a brutal show of force, recalls the horrors

3 See "A Wild And Far-Fetched Idea," page 79.
4 Barack Obama, "Remarks by the President on the Middle East and North Africa," *The White House*, May 19, 2011. http://www.whitehouse.gov/the-press-office/2011/05/19/remarks-president-middle-east-and-north-africa.
5 "Assad gives mixed signals in speech," *Al Jazeera*, June 20, 2011, http://www.aljazeera.com/news/middleeast/2011/06/201162084915169403.html.

of the infamous 1982 massacre at Hama. Yet, whereas Bashar's father Hafez was then successful in using overwhelming violence to quiet dissent, signs of military mutiny today suggest that any success by Assad in quelling the unrest will be short-lived. It will be only a matter of time before the Syrian youth rise again, except this time no force, however brutal, will be able to suppress them.

As in Tunisia and Egypt, once the military turns on the government, its downfall becomes imminent. While the Syrian military's commanders are from Assad's ruling-minority Alawite sect, most conscripts are Sunni. These soldiers know that they are under careful watch for any signs of dissent, which carry lethal consequences. But as the indiscriminate violence against civilians grows and the military is stretched too thin, there are strong indications that soldiers will begin to defect en masse, and Assad's regime will finally reach the brink of collapse.

Of course, Assad will do everything in his power to avoid such a scenario. The provocative marching of Syrians to the border with Israel a few weeks ago is just one indication of Assad's need to distract attention from the atrocities occurring in his country. As Assad becomes desperate, he could resort to a more direct confrontation with Israel, believing that a Syrian-Israeli conflict could unite the Syrian people in support of his government. But this is a delusion. Assad can no longer expect to deceive the Syrian people, who will delight at the fall of his regime. Assad might also increase support for terror acts that could deviate attention from Damascus, while seeking greater assistance from Iran and its nearby proxy, Hezbollah. But this too could serve as an invitation to Israel to finish off his regime. Soon, Assad will realize that he has no options left, and he may regret not living up to his empty promises of reform. He may also realize that the only way in which he will be allowed to die as the ruler of Syria, like his father, is if he dies at the hands of the enraged Syrian citizenry.

It is no longer a question if Bashar al-Assad will fall—it is a question of when. Now the matter becomes what happens after Assad leaves. Syria's dissatisfied and conflicting sects (Alawite, Sunni, Kurd, and Shi'ite, among others), devoid of strong leadership, could be the recipe for a disaster. With the Alawites making up just over 10 percent of the Syrian population, the retribution against the elites could be severe. Already, sectarian violence has sparked in the country. The economic plunge that is accompanying the current unrest will only exacerbate these tensions further. In the absence of any authority, Iran and the terror groups it supports will be in a unique position to consolidate their influence within the country. With Assad leaning heavily on the Islamic Republic, Iran has a unique window into the current dynamics in Syria which the Western world does not. Furthermore, it is conceivable that Iran would deploy Hezbollah, or even its own troops, in an effort to save the Assad regime or to install one that is favorable to the interests of Tehran. Faced with the strengthening of Iranian influence along its border, the potential for a renewed Israel-Hezbollah clash could intensify. Meanwhile, with refugees flooding Turkey, Ankara may intrude on Syrian territory to stem the tide of unrest from crossing the Turkey-Syria border. The instability and uncertainty that will follow the fall of Assad is likely to mirror Iraqi or Lebanese sectarian warfare, complicated by neighboring states like Israel and Iran who will take action to ensure security needs or even to fill the power vacuum.

The question that emerges now is how can Syria be eased from Assad's grasp without descending into chaos? Opposition groups have met in Turkey seeking to coalesce into a 31-member transitional council that would serve as a governing body able to steward Syria from Assad's regime to a democratic state. However, no visible leader has emerged. The efforts to make a unified opposition still prove to be weak; a recent meeting in Damascus produced no results and only invited criticism from outside opposition. This is because until a few months ago, there was virtually no Syrian opposition, as it had been stamped out entirely by the Assad regime. This complicates the newly formed opposition's efforts. So too does the fact that the various figures in this opposition, representing the various Syrian sects, have little in common beyond a desire to see the overthrow of the Assad government. Furthermore, the uprising has largely been led by young people who are likely unaware of opposition dissidents who are abroad and not participating in the day-to-day battles with Assad's forces, but who could cause discord as efforts unfold.

The challenges facing the formation of any shadow government are large. But if the opposition is to succeed, it will need the support of the international community. Today, the international community is failing miserably to do anything about the slaughter of the Syrian people. The Arab League has long been without influence in Damascus, with Assad choosing to align himself with Tehran against the wishes of his Arab counterparts. But the lack of any Arab voice standing up for the Syrian people has been shameful. Whereas the Arab League played a critical role in calling for the ousting of Muammar al-Qaddafi, with regard to Syria, the only benign statement that Arab League chief and Egyptian presidential candidate Amr Moussa could recently muster was that "there is a worry in the Arab world and in the region concerning the events in Syria."[6]

The lack of Arab leadership only makes the likelihood that Iran will pick up the pieces upon Assad's fall even greater. Meanwhile, the United States has not done any

---

6 "Syrian tanks enter Turkey border village," *AFP*, June 18, 2011. http://www.google.com/
   hostednews/afp/article/ALeqM5gNgiQ1p_6m6T7bAugobdbv-UBZrQ?docId=CNG.
   d08b4e3cb5e105e6a0b700a119dd138f.471.

better. Now three months into the uprising, the United States has yet to directly call for Assad's ousting, and has not so much as withdrawn the U.S. Ambassador from Damascus. Its inability to act has further diminished American credibility and influence in the region while increasingly appearing hypocritical and weak. Together with France and Britain, the United States has been unable to advance a resolution condemning Syria at the United Nations. Russia and China, in a new low for international diplomacy, shamefully refuse to even discuss the matter, as dozens of Syrians die each day.

So what can be done? The United States and those in the international community, including the European Union, who presume to stand up for the rights of the Syrian people, must create policies that combine coercive actions and quiet diplomacy to oust Assad and lay the groundwork for a less volatile future for the Syrian nation. This must include new crippling sanctions targeting a much broader swath of Syrian officials and robust support for the nascent Syrian opposition movement. It should also include diplomacy that offers Assad and his cronies a way to relinquish power in exchange for asylum before sending the nation into prolonged chaos and destruction. Turkey can play an especially vital role in these efforts.

Turkey-Syria ties have strengthened in recent years, with open borders and increased trade. But after once calling Assad his "brother," newly re-elected Prime Minister Recep Tayyip Erdogan has publicly admonished the Syrian government, recently stating that the troops in the Syrian army's 4th division, commanded by Assad's brother Maher, "don't behave like humans."[7] In addition, after a recent phone conversation with Syrian leadership, Erdogan lamented that the regime was taking the situation "lightly." Turkish influence in Syria, as well as its stakes in a stable Syria, is considerable. And with Turkey's desire to play a leadership role in the region, now could be time for the United States and the Europeans to further encourage Turkey to do so by serving as a mediator to bring Assad, and Syria, away from further catastrophe.

Bashar al-Assad once held promise as a young Arab leader at the cross-section of the Middle East, promising reform and holding many of the keys to stability, security, peace and prosperity in the region. He has squandered all of his opportunities. Instead of leadership, he has shown a new level of arrogance and brutality. The obnoxious belief of the Assad clan and his counterparts in Libya and Yemen that they can rule in perpetuity without a modicum of consent by their respective people is nothing short of revolting. Assad may not be allowing journalists to enter Syria, but the world is indeed watching –and he can no longer hide his brutality. Sadly, it remains to be seen whether world leaders are capable of doing anything about it.

---

7 "Erdogan: Syrian troops barbaric, 'don't behave like humans'," *Jerusalem Post*, June 10, 2011, http://www.jpost.com/Middle-East/Erdogan-Syrian-troops-barbaric-dont-behave-like-humans.

ASSAD'S DEMISE, IRANIAN SHADOWS

NOVEMBER 22, 2011

Unlike any other Arab country, Syria holds the key to several conflicts in the Middle East. The future of the Iran-led "resistance block" (along with Syria, Hezbollah, and Hamas), stabilization in Iraq, the conflict with Israel, as well as Turkey's "new eastern policy" all depend on what will happen in Syria in the wake of the ongoing uprising. Now, after eight months of protests, with thousands of people killed, tens of thousands arrested and no end in sight, what can be done to stop the carnage and inhibit, if not end, Iran's direct intervention to keep Assad in power and extricate Tehran from Damascus through a regime change? A general look at the scene suggests six major elements that characterize the current situation in Syria which make it unlikely for Syria's President Assad to stay in power.

First, as the crackdown continues, international sanctions, though still far from crippling the regime, have started to drain the regime's economic as well as diplomatic resources. Oil revenues will dry up as export contracts largely expired in mid-November after the European Union implemented a ban on Syrian oil. Turkey, which has held the United States from taking action against Damascus in the hope that Assad will make reforms, has also finally abandoned Assad. Not only has Turkey hosted the establishment of the Syrian National Council (SNC) by opposition groups in Istanbul, but Turkey is also currently conducting military exercises on the Syrian border, with plans in place for a possible occupation of northern Syria to provide a safe haven for refugees and military defectors escaping the killing.[8]

Second, the regime has lost legitimacy and is unlikely to restore it. Unlike democracies, authoritarian regimes can still maintain legitimacy through means other than being elected as representatives of their people, particularly by providing basic public goods and services. Assad's loss of legitimacy was not, therefore, from failing to lead a democratic transition, as President Obama stated in mid-July,[9] but the result of the regime's gradual failure to deliver public goods, and later the indiscriminate killing of its citizens, especially when the sanctions continue to undermine the patron-client relationship that the regime has maintained for decades with the business elite.

Third, the majority of the Syrian people are being increasingly alienated. It is not unusual for authoritarian regimes to face dissent, but the ability to crush protests

---

8 Ayla Albayrak, "Turkey Is Adding to Pressure on Damascus," *The Wall Street Journal*, October 5, 2011, http://online.wsj.com/article/SB10001424052970204524604576610781937462842.html.
9 "Obama Says Assad Has 'Lost Legitimacy'," *Radio Free Europe*, July 13, 2011, http://www.rferl.org/content/obama_says_assad_has_lost_legitimacy/24263894.html.

is always situation-specific. In 1982, Bashar Assad's father, Hafez, quelled a revolt in the city of Hama by killing an estimated 20,000 of its residents, and his regime survived for two more decades. In 2011, the recurrent, though qualified, victories of Arab revolutions as well as the media scrutiny (social media in particular) have emboldened the protesters and restricted the regime. Even if the protest is crushed now, the hatred that the government's violence has fed makes it only a matter of time before protests are resurrected with even greater force.

Fourth, the prospect of a civil war looms large on the horizon. Syria's Alawite ruling minority and the Sunnis are becoming mortal enemies. Random killings of civilians are committed not only by government forces but also by members of the Sunni and the Alawite communities against one another. With the rising toll of civilian deaths, protesters are becoming more militant and people on both sides are buying weapons which are being smuggled in from Lebanon for self-defense and offensive operations. Uncontained, such a situation runs the high risk of turning into another post-Saddam Iraq, where vendettas prevail between the Sunni and Shiites.

Fifth, there is military defection. Though figures have not been quantified accurately, there is no question that a growing number of the Syrian military's rank-and-file (mostly Sunni) are now defecting for refusing to shoot their fellow countrymen. This is a very bad omen for the regime. Not only is defection contagious, threatening the coherence of the regime's backbone, but there is the likely chance that these combat-trained soldiers could soon form the base of an organized, armed opposition supported by the international community, paving the way for regime change *à la* Libya.

Sixth, the Arab initiative to end the violence in Syria has reached an impasse. On November 12th, the Arab League suspended Syria and imposed political and economic sanctions at their Cairo meeting due to the Syrian government's continued violence against protesters. After nearly two weeks of wrangling between the two sides, Damascus and the Arab Foreign Ministers failed to agree on a plan that would permit 500 monitors to enter the country. The Arab states rejected what it saw as Syrian efforts to drastically change the Arab League's peace blueprint, which also called on the Syrian government to immediately remove troops from cities and towns and conduct negotiations with the opposition. The failure to reach an agreement made it more than likely that the Arab League would recognize the opposition in Syria, once unified, as the sole representative of the Syrian people, very similar to Libya's National Transitional Council.

Combined, these elements lead to the conclusion that it is already too late for the Assad regime to make reforms or lead a transition in Syria. Though practically doomed, the regime, the Alawite elite, the military, and the internal security forces remain resilient and generally united and will almost certainly persist in the crackdown, in what they see as a fight for their own lives and tinged with the unrealistic hope that the tide can still change in their favor.

The international community cannot sit aloof while the massacre continues in Syria, as a largely peaceful demonstration is not likely to succeed in toppling the government on its own. Thousands of Syrian people will continue to be killed either at the hands of Assad's security forces or in sectarian violence. Meanwhile, a Libyan-like international military intervention does not appear feasible as the United States (in the midst of presidential elections) and the EU have no desire to get involved in yet another Middle East conflict, especially one laden with dangerous geopolitical complications and unforeseen consequences.

A coherent strategy is urgently needed to ensure the fall of the Syrian regime and the strengthening of the democracy-seeking protests in Syria while substantially eroding Iran's grip on Damascus.

First, fearing that he may meet Qaddafi's fate and concerned that he may never regain the legitimacy needed to lead, President Assad *might* be willing to negotiate a safe passage and immunity from prosecution for himself, his family, Alawite leaders, and several dozen of his top military, internal security, and intelligence personnel. This is particularly urgent as it would need to occur before Assad and his brother are indicted by the International Criminal Court, which can happen as soon as charges of *en masse* killing are brought against them. Once Assad is indicted (and fearing that he will be caught and stand trial), he will be discouraged from opting for this course. For this reason, the Obama administration, in consultation with its allies (in particular Turkey), should fully and aggressively explore this option with key Arab states (in particular Saudi Arabia and Qatar) to identify where Assad might find safe haven and spare his country from racing ever so rapidly toward the abyss.

Should these efforts fail, then other severe measures must be considered. The international community will have to intensify the sanctions on Syria. With or without a new Security Council resolution, the US and the EU must make sure to close all the loopholes and make the sanctions smart enough to target the Syrian leadership and its ability to utilize its weapons and communications systems. Moreover, failing to reach an agreement with the Arab League (in particular Saudi Arabia, Egypt, and the UAE, whose merchandise exchange with Syria is close to 40% of its international trade)[10] means they are now more likely to impose their own sanctions similar to Turkey.

10 "Syria," *CIA World Factbook*, accessed November 20, 2011. https://www.cia.gov/library/publications/the-world-factbook/geos/sy.html.

The United States and the EU should help (and at the same time pressure) the newly formed Syrian National Council (SNC) to become a more organized and representative body of the Syrian people and its political, ethnic, and religious mosaic. The SNC must close ranks, offer a clear vision of a future Syria and an unambiguous alternative to the current regime with a specific agenda, and form a "shadow government." Indeed, for the Syrian people to rally around the SNC they must have a clear sense of where and how such a body is planning to lead Syria post-Assad. An empowered SNC, viewed as a viable alternative which demonstrates cohesiveness and the capability to manage a peaceful transition, could then receive international recognition and support (already offered by Turkey and foreshadowed by the Arab League), which would further embolden the protesters, galvanize Assad's illegitimacy to rule, and speed his departure.

The US should lead a coordinated effort to provide material support through Turkey to the protesters. While not necessarily arms, certainly logistical support, aid, and protection for the besieged communities along the lines of the Berlin Airlift of 1948-9 would be in order. Facing the full fury of the regime's security machine, Syrian protesters need to fight in self-defense and feed their families. If the international community cannot help with the former, it certainly can with the latter. Moreover, to silence Syria's air-defense system, the United States needs not launch air strikes but could instead employ cyber-warfare, an option it considered against Qaddafi's Libya.[11]

Perhaps most important is the Iran factor that has become extraordinarily more worrisome to the US and its allies, as the Syrian regime is becoming increasingly more dependent on Iran's material, logistical, and military support. For Iran, maintaining its grip on Damascus is central to its ambitions to become the region's hegemon, exercising unprecedented influence over a contiguous landmass extending from the Persian Gulf to the Mediterranean, especially as Tehran is coming closer to acquiring nuclear weapons. This dimension has far-reaching implications for the security of the US and its allies in the Gulf and presents an imperative, historic opportunity for the US and the Gulf governments to ensure a transition of power in Syria.

Only through a regime change in Damascus will Iran's exploitation of Syria's heterogeneous make up in pursuit of its hegemonic ambitions (as it has, and continues to do, in Iraq) be stopped. A stalwart suspension of Syria by the Arab League would, no doubt, open the door for bolder Western intervention to further isolate the Assad leadership and send a clear message to Iran that it will not be allowed to have a free hand in Syria.

11 Eric Schmitt and Thom Shanker, "U.S. Debated Cyberwarfare in Attack Plan on Libya," *The New York Times*, October 17, 2011. http://www.nytimes.com/2011/10/18/world/africa/cyber-warfare-against-libya-was-debated-by-us.html?_r=0.

The choice between "Assad-or-chaos" is no longer relevant, if it has ever been. The US with its European allies, especially Turkey, must now muster all possible means to end the slaughter in Syria. It is certainly a tall and most complicated order. There is, however, no other viable option that would also limit, if not end, Iran's direct involvement in keeping Assad in power and spare the region from a potential war that could involve Iran and Israel.

HOW SYRIA'S RULING APPARATUS BECAME ITS ALBATROSS

JANUARY 30, 2012

It was strongly suggested by top officials in the Syrian government that I spoke with more than a decade ago that when Syria's President, Bashar Assad, first assumed power he was determined to introduce some significant political reforms. Why then has he failed to implement at least some of what he had intended to do and failed to meet the public's expectations for change following his father's 30-year reign? The reason is that Mr. Assad inherited from his father more than merely the office of the Presidency. He inherited a system of governing—an entrenched ruling apparatus consisting of the Ba'ath party leadership, the high military brass, a massive intelligence (Mukhabarat) community, internal security, and top business elites—all dominated by Bashar's own Alawite minority group which had heavily-vested interests in maintaining the system at all costs. Mr. Assad was able to assert his rule based only on the tacit condition that he would preserve the status quo, which in the end turned out to be his albatross.

At the onset of the upheaval nearly ten months ago, Mr. Assad was again inclined to make some concessions to pacify the people but was immediately overruled by the same clique of powerful individuals that surround him today, including his powerful brother, Maher, the commander of the Republican Guard. The same inter-play is currently taking place as elements of the ruling apparatus have tied their fates together with the knowledge that meaningful reforms would inevitably usurp many of their powers which they are unwilling to relinquish, regardless of the public's suffering. For this reason, any practical solution to Syria's crisis must take into account the nature of its intra-group relations and the choices that can be made within such relations.

The failure of the Arab League (AL) observers' mission was predictable as they did not have the mandate or the ability to move freely anywhere within the country, being instead directed by the Syrian authorities to visit and report about places and incidents of the government's choosing. From the start of the observers' mission a month ago, government forces have killed more than five hundred Syrians.[12] Following the extension of the mission by an additional month only a few days ago,[13] the Arab League decided to suspend the observers' mission as the indiscriminate killing of civilians

12 Alexandra Zavis and Rima Marrouch, "Comment by chief of Arab League observers in Syria is criticized," *Los Angeles Times*, December 29, 2011, http://articles.latimes.com/2011/dec/29/world/la-fg-syria-observers-20111229.
13 "Syria agrees to extend Arab League observer mission," *BBC News*, January 24, 2012, http://www.bbc.co.uk/news/world-16708348.

continued. Neither the continuation of such a mission (which was already thwarted after all of the Gulf states' observers quit) nor the call by the AL for Assad to step down for new assembly elections within two months to draft a new constitution would bring about any serious change. The AL decision to turn to the UN with the support of the US and the EU at the time of this writing may produce a watered down resolution at best that will neither call for Assad to step down nor impose any meaningful sanctions. Russia has already made it abundantly clear that it will veto any such resolution.

Considering the fact that whatever happens in Syria will have serious regional repercussions, any outside interference will have to be carefully weighed against the internal conditions and how they are evolving. One thing, however, remains clear: significant and permanent changes will not occur in Syria through any kind of give and take with the current government, as the problem is not Assad himself so much as the clique surrounding him which will remain even if he steps down. In this regard, the AL, with the support of other major players including Turkey, should develop a strategy that will squeeze out Assad and his cohorts, even though this may still take the better part of 2012. The strategy should consist of four distinct yet interconnected components, which should be pursued simultaneously.

First, fearing that he may meet Qaddafi's fate and concerned that he may never regain the legitimacy needed to lead, an offer to negotiate a safe exit and immunity from prosecution for himself, his family, Alawite leaders and several dozens of his lieutenants should be placed on the table. This is particularly urgent as it would need to occur before Assad and his clique are indicted by the International Criminal Court, which can happen as soon as charges of *en masse* killing are brought against them. Once Assad is indicted, he will be discouraged from opting for this course. For this reason, instead of asking Assad to hand over power to one deputy (a plan already rejected and dubbed a "plot" by Syria's Foreign Minister, Walid al-Muallem),[14] the AL, in consultation with the Obama administration and Turkey, should fully and aggressively explore the "safe exit" option where Assad is offered a safe haven, sparing his country from racing further toward the abyss. The "safe exit" option has already worked in Yemen, and the Saudi Royal family would not object to allowing Assad and his clique sanctuary, as it did earlier with Uganda's Idi Amin and more recently with Tunisia's Zine El Abidine Ben Ali.

Second, Assad may not opt for the first option, anticipating that Iran and Russia will keep him well-equipped and well-financed and hoping to crush the uprising. Therefore, a joint effort should be made by the AL, the United States, the European

14 Alistair Lyon, "Arab League turns to U.N. as Gulf observers quit Syria," *Reuters*, January 24, 2012. http://www.reuters.com/article/2012/01/24/us-syria-idUSTRE8041A820120124.

Union, and Turkey to impose crippling sanctions. These sanctions should include: cutting off all civilian flights, ending trade with several Arab trading partners (including Jordan and Saudi Arabia), threatening to intervene militarily through no-fly zones, and enlisting the use of cyber warfare. Unlike Iraq, an almost completely self-sustained country, Syria desperately depends on imports. Sanctions like these would be very painful and might pressure the entire ruling apparatus to gradually collapse. The UN Security Council is currently considering an Arab-European draft resolution reflecting the demands of the AL initiative, which calls for Assad to hand power over to his deputy but mentions no use of sanctions as a consequence of non-compliance. Despite Russian objections to the draft, Moscow may eventually relent with some US inducement. As a senior Russian envoy has been quoted this week, "Russia can do no more [for Assad]"[15]—something that should serve as a serious signal to Assad.

Third, as the first two prongs of the strategy are initiated, the high military command should be encouraged to mount a military coup. Such a coup could gather momentum as the military high brass could conclude that, given the rising defections and the state's failure to repress the year-long protests so far, even undertaking massacres on the scale of Hama in February of 1982 would not turn the tide. The military command may then seriously consider the Egyptian model where the military high brass, motivated by its own survival, opted for abandoning Mubarak and his immediate associates, while promising and implementing real reforms. The Syrian military remains the strongest institution within the country and possesses the capability to impose its will. For its high command, the option of sacrificing Assad and some two dozen of his cohorts as the symbol of tyranny would maintain the unity of the army and, above all, save the lives and interests of the bulk of the ruling apparatus. This scenario may have been unlikely only a few months ago partly because of the military's loyalty to Assad's Alawite community and partly because of the regime's security firewalls, which have prevented a military coup in Syria for the last four decades. But now the conditions on the ground have changed in a dramatic way and only a dramatic move will stop the carnage in a situation which is steadily leading towards a civil war.

Finally, for all intents and purposes, the sectarian conflict has already begun and will likely, if unimpeded, turn into a full-scale civil war. Should this scenario unfold, it will eventually bring down the Assad regime, and no one in his current power structure will survive. The initially limited defections are now in the hundreds every single day, which has allowed for the emergence of the Free Syrian Army (FSA) as an organized and armed opposition practically working as the military wing of the Syrian National Council. The FSA is in control of two key cities, Douma (on the north-east edge of Damascus) and

15 "Russia: We can do no more for Syria's Assad," *NBC News*, January 23, 2012. http://worldnews. nbcnews.com/_news/2012/01/23/10217332-russia-we-can-do-no-more-for-syrias-assad.

Zabadani (close to the Lebanese border), which has forced the regime into indirect nego-tiations to stop the fighting.[16] Should this scenario unfold it will likely follow the Libyan model of capturing one city after another, resulting in slaughter, especially given recent reports that the regime has already started distributing weapons in the country's Alawite areas with the double aim of denying the FSA further gains and targeting the silent ma-jority's fear of sectarian divides *à la* post-Saddam Iraq.[17]

Time has run out for President Assad. Following the mass killings, suffering, and deprivation of basic human rights that the Assad regime has perpetrated, under no circumstances will Assad be able to restore his legitimacy as a ruler either externally or domestically, even if some calm is re-established. Ironically, Assad, who might have been the first leader in Syria who actually wanted to institute some political reforms, might very well end up being the first to be sacrificed because of the governing ap-paratus he inherited but failed to upend. The Assad dynasty as we know it will most definitely be a thing of the past, regardless of how long that may take.

16 "Indirect negotiations taking place between FSA and regime – Rebel commander," *Asharq al-Awsat*, January 27, 2012. http://www.aawsat.net/2012/01/article55243435.
17 "Khaddam: Assad's strategic weapons at unknown place," *LBCI*, January 26, 2012. http://www.lbcgroup.tv/news/18312/khaddam-assads-strategic-weapons-at-unknown-place.

END THE SLAUGHTER IN SYRIA WHILE ISOLATING IRAN

FEBRUARY 20, 2012

Seldom has the dividing line between the forces of moderation and the forces of extremism been so clear in the Middle East. The extremist anti-West, Iran-led Shiite Crescent, consisting of Iraq (largely operating at Iran's behest), Syria, and Lebanon, heavily subsidized by Tehran with political capital and financial resources for the past three decades, is now under serious threat of collapse thanks to the crack in its most critical link: Syria's Assad regime. On the other hand, the human tragedy in Syria has created a rare common interest between the old and the new Arab regimes, Turkey, the US, and the EU for the potential emergence of a representative government in Damascus.

Nonetheless, while Iran, Russia, and China are doing their utmost to prevent the fall of Assad, the international and regional forces of moderation have yet to rise up to the challenge. Unless this loose alliance of moderate forces closes ranks and embarks on a decisive effort to break the Shiite Crescent, the Syrian people will be left alone to face a continuing massacre and will miss a historic opportunity to join a new, peaceful, and potentially more democratically-oriented Middle East. Turkey especially stands to gain from a more vigorous involvement of the forces of moderation.

On February 16th, the United Nations General Assembly (UNGA) voted overwhelmingly for a resolution backing the Arab League's (AL) plan calling for Bashar Assad to step down and strongly condemned the widespread and systematic human rights violations committed by his forces, further demanding that the government immediately cease all acts of violence. Although the UNGA resolution is not binding, it offers powerful moral support to the Syrian opposition, especially after the Russian-Chinese veto earlier this month of a United Nations Security Council (UNSC) resolution to the same effect. Equally, the UNGA resolution strongly fortifies the moral standing that enables the AL, Turkey and the West to venture beyond their current tentative positions, given the apparent failure of all other initiatives thus far.

The AL initiative, calling for a transfer of power to Syrian Vice President Farouk al-Shara'a, the formation of a unity government, and the referral of this initiative to the UNSC to assist in its implementation, has been dysfunctional from the beginning. A transfer of power to the Syrian VP, even if the initiative had passed in the UNSC, would deliver zero change in Syria given that al-Shara'a himself has been a prominent member of Syria's ruling apparatus for almost thirty years. A similar "VP scenario" proposed by the Saudi-led Gulf Cooperation Council managed (though by no means perfectly) to defuse an explosion in Yemen. But whereas the removal of Yemen's President Ali Abdullah Saleh has persuaded the Yemeni public, the problem in Syria is not with Bashar Assad *per se* but with the entire government apparatus within which he is encased. That is why the AL needs to avoid symbolic actions and face the reality on the ground, however bitter and unsettling it may be.

The other AL initiative calling for the UNSC to create a joint UN-Arab peacekeeping force for Syria, even in the unlikely event that it passes in the UN veto-controlled body, amounts to nothing more than another exercise in futility. For starters, there is no peace to keep in Syria. Suffice it to recall the failures of UN peacekeepers in Rwanda, Bosnia, and the Congo to point to the UN's inability to fill such a role in the absence of both peace and cooperation between the conflicting parties on the ground. Sending a UN peacekeeping mission to Syria at this time would only help the Assad regime stay in power even longer. Also, such a UN mission would most likely meet the same fate as the recently-withdrawn AL observers, whose activities were controlled by the Syrian authorities and ended up playing into the hands of the regime. The observers stood idle while the massacres continued before the AL decided to suspend their mission. The UN peacekeeping force would have to be under the control of the UNSC rather than under that of the Syrian government, mandated by the UNSC to move freely throughout Syria and report with no restrictions on the unfolding events. But then again, the Syrian government is not likely to allow such a force to enter Syria, which could only further embolden the resistance to Assad's rule while restricting the governments' retaliations.

Finally, the reforms introduced by the Assad government, such as holding a referendum on a new constitution as well as parliamentary elections, are merely ploys aimed at buying more time. Therefore, it should come as no surprise that these bogus reforms have been supported by Russia and more recently by China. These reforms will not be accepted by the Syrian people who have sacrificed so much only to settle for the scraps exacted under duress from a government that has lost its bearings and credibility and whose removal the people demand. Assad and his cohorts refused to make a solid commitment, they were engaged in protracted negotiations to dilute any meaningful reforms, and subsequently were involved in systematic prevarication – all the while persisting in violent crackdowns. Syria's problem lies not in the wording of its laws, but in the very regime that drafts and implements these laws.

The forthcoming AL meeting in Tunisia on February 24 should capitalize on the powerful message sent by the 137 nations at the UNGA condemning the Syrian security forces' onslaught on its people while providing moral support that goes beyond polemics and opens the door for real action on the ground. The members of the moderate camp should implement such bold measures as the establishment of a "Freedom

Corridor" by carving out a portion of Syrian territory in the north bordering Turkey. As in Libya, a no-fly zone air-patrolled by willing NATO and AL member states should be established immediately over this corridor, but without engaging in combat with the government forces, except in defense of the corridor.

This corridor would provide a humanitarian safe haven for civilian refugees escaping the violence and would receive military defectors while serving as a base for arming the Free Syrian Army as Senators John McCain and Lindsey Graham, both of whom serve on the Senate Armed Services Committee, have recently advocated. Moreover, the corridor will allow the Syrian National Council (SNC) to place a foot on Syrian ground, thereby paving the way for its recognition by the AL and Western and Muslim powers. In addition, the SNC should establish a shadow government composed of non-ideological professionals and technocrats to begin planning for a post-Assad era. NATO members, particularly France (which already advanced the idea of a humanitarian air corridor last November), as well as the AL are likely to support such a proposal.

Israel can quietly contribute by opening and monitoring closely its Syrian border for refugees from southern Syria for whom the advocated northern safety zone is beyond their reach. This Israeli action can be done in coordination with Jordan, which shares borders with both Syria and Israel. But the largest responsibility lies with Turkey, with the full support of the Arab League.

Of all the moderate camp members, Turkey is the largest stakeholder in Syria. Short of an intervention by the international community, the current conflict in Syria will soon turn into a full-scale civil war that will flood Turkey with refugees, empower the PKK base in northern Syria, and secure an enlarged Iranian influence in its immediate proximity, all to Turkey's disadvantage. At the same time, Turkey is best located geographically and politically to allow and support the establishment of this corridor along its southeastern border. A Turkey that takes the initiative would not only demonstrate true leadership in the Middle East and further strengthen its alliance with the West, but would also bridge its relations with an Arab world that has become increasingly worried about a neo-Ottoman foreign policy in the region. For Ankara, it is time to reconcile with the bitter reality that there is no middle ground: either stop Iran in Syria and stop the massacre or surrender Syria to Iran's domain, thereby further encouraging Iran to pursue its ambition of becoming the region's hegemon, potentially equipped with nuclear capabilities.

For all intents and purposes, Syria has turned into the battleground between the forces of moderation and the forces of extremism in the Middle East. Feeble attempts by the international community will lead nowhere as long as they ignore the realities of the Ba'athist regime in Syria. At the same time, any prospect of reaching some kind of an arrangement agreed upon by Assad that is meant to empower the Syrian people is an illusion. However, removing Syria from Iran's grasp while freeing the Syrian people from Assad's shackles will have dramatic geopolitical implications as it will also change the power equation throughout the Middle East. To be sure, decoupling Syria from Iran's hold would further underline the regional and international isolation of Tehran and might avert military action against Iran by either Israel or the U.S., the aim of which would be to end its nuclear ambitions.

The victory of Iran & Co. in Syria would be catastrophic for the region and should be stopped, given the opportunity currently available. By ensuring a regime change supportive of the Syrian people's yearning for freedom, the Shiite Crescent would be broken and place insurmountable pressure on Iran to end its meddling in the affairs of its Arab neighbors.

ALON BEN-MEIR

SYRIAN KURDS: TIME TO ASSERT THEIR RIGHTS

MARCH 27, 2012

Regardless of what may come out of Kofi Annan's peace plan to end the internal conflict in Syria, and whatever may emerge from the Arab League meeting this week in Baghdad, the prospect of Assad's fall offers the Kurdish minority in Syria a historic opportunity to gain equal political and civil rights. Given the totalitarian nature of Baathist rule under Assad, the regime's fall in Syria will take the entire system of government down with it, much like Saddam's Iraq in 2003. But unlike Iraq's Kurds, who have enjoyed virtual autonomy since 1991 when the United States enforced a no-fly zone over northern Iraq, Syria's Kurds are less organized and more divided. Syrian Kurds need to close ranks, fully join the Syrian people in pursuit of freedom, and not allow this historic window of opportunity to slip away.

Unless it wishes to preside over a divided Syria where the Kurds could contribute to prolonged instability, any elected government emerging in post-Assad Syria must commit itself to the equality of all Syrian citizens, regardless of their ethnic background. The Kurdish nation constitutes a population of more than 40 million people, the majority of whom live on a contiguous landmass that includes Iraq, Iran, Turkey, and Syria.[18] The Kurds are the world's largest minority group that remains stateless. The nearly century-old denial of equal political and civil rights for Kurds in these four countries has been a contentious issue with all Kurdish minorities ever since the Kurdish territory was divided after World War I between Iraq, Iran, Turkey, and Syria, with the sole exception of the short-lived Kingdom of Kurdistan from September 1922 to July 1924 when the Kurds enjoyed political independence.[19] Although in all host countries the Kurds are discriminated against in varying degrees, their living conditions in Syria are even worse as many are denied citizenship, land ownership, and even the freedom of movement within the country.

To fully gain from the popular revolt and achieve equal rights with the rest of the Syrian people, Syria's Kurds need to take five central steps and remain consistent and unwavering, regardless of how treacherous the road to freedom may be.

First, they must organize themselves and develop a coherent agenda, which they can use to advance from the early stages of the revolution until President Assad is deposed and

---

18 Dieter Farwick, "The Kurds: one nation in four countries," World Security Network, April 19, 2011, http://www.worldsecuritynetwork.com/Religion-and-Politics-Peace-and-Conflict-Human-Rights-Europe-Broader-Middle-East/dieter-farwick-1/The-Kurds-one-nation-in-four-countries.

19 Wadie Jwaideh, *The Kurdish National Movement: Its Origins and Developments* (Syracuse, NY: Syracuse University Press, 2006), 192-202.

the country moves toward clear reforms. The Syrian Kurds need to assert themselves as an integral part of the Syrian population and identify with the Syrian people's just and non-violent struggle to remove the regime and elect a government committed to the universal values of freedom, human rights, and democracy. The Syrian Kurds should not, at this juncture, seek either the establishment of a federal system or strive for an autonomous region. Instead, they should commit themselves to Syria's unity and its constitutional laws, which will be collectively enacted by a new parliament.

Second, rival Kurdish groups must end their deep divisions and present a unified approach if they want to be recognized and dealt with seriously. The Kurdistan Democratic Party of Syria (KDPS) supports the removal of the Assad regime while the Democratic Union Party (PYD), which has close ties to Turkey's PKK, is concerned that Assad's removal will lead to the dominance of the Turkish-supported Muslim Brotherhood, which would maintain the same anti-Kurd policy.[20] The Assad regime is currently exploiting the Kurdish division by allowing the PYD leadership to return from exile while permitting it to open Kurdish language schools, cultural centers, and party offices in Syrian cities. The success of the Syrian Kurds in achieving true equality will ultimately depend on their ability to unite, and remain united, throughout the revolutionary process. PYD leadership must be reminded that its pro-Assad approach is a losing strategy in either case: if the regime survives, however unlikely, it will not hesitate to revoke all of the concessions it has made in times of crisis, and if the regime falls, which is more likely, the new government will probably settle the account (for supporting Assad) with the PYD and the Kurds.

Third, the leadership of the Kurds must demand and insist on proportional representation within the Syrian National Council (SNC). Currently there is only one delegate, which is hardly representative of the size of the Kurdish community in Syria, which constitutes 10-12% of Syria's total population (around two million people).[21] While KDPS, the SNC's main Kurdish component, should work harder to convince other reluctant parties, particularly the PYD, to join forces, the SNC should be aware that it could also significantly benefit from broader Kurdish representation if it wants to be seriously representative of the Syrian people and its political, ethnic, and religious mosaic. Shortchanging the Kurds will undoubtedly raise serious concerns among other minorities within the country, such as the Armenians, the Druze, and other groups, that will fear similar marginalization within the new Syria.

---

20 Othman Ali, "The struggle for the hearts of Kurds in Syria: Barzani vs. Öcalan," *Today's Zaman*, February 13, 2012, http://www.todayszaman.com/news-271327-the-struggle-for-the-hearts-of-kurds-in-syria-barzani-vs-ocalan-by-othman-ali*.html.

21 Harvey Morris, "Turkish Worries Over Syria Blamed on 'Kurdish Phobia'," *International Herald Tribune*, July 31, 2012, http://rendezvous.blogs.nytimes.com/2012/07/31/inside-turkey-concern-over-kurdish-phobia-around-syria/.

Fourth, the Kurdish leadership should approach their relationship with Turkey with caution. Since the SNC is headquartered in Istanbul, it is certainly influenced by the Erdogan government, which does not want, for obvious reasons, to encourage federal or autonomous solutions for the Kurds. Syria's Kurds have every reason to question Turkey's intentions because Ankara clearly wants to see the Muslim Brotherhood, with which it has a close affinity, in power in Damascus. Moreover, the Kurds do not rule out a possible Turkish military intervention in Syria to ensure stability. Such an intervention will still be used to solidify the dominance of the MB. Nevertheless, the Syrian Kurdish leadership should cooperate and enhance its relations with Turkey not only because it is premature for Syria's divided Kurds to challenge Turkey's plan but also because the Kurds' sole other option is anathema: an Assad regime that is closer than ever to Iran.

Finally, the Syrian Kurds should learn from, and ask for the support of, their brethren, the Iraqi Kurds, who benefited greatly from the fall of Saddam Hussein and are currently running the Kurdistan region as a prosperous island of stability within a conflict-torn Iraq. Since affinity between the Kurds (regardless of their country of residence) is stronger than the affinity to their separate host states, Iraq's Kurdistan Region is a natural ally and is freer to help the Kurds' cause in Syria in contrast to the Iraqi government, which tacitly supports Assad. Syria's Kurds can benefit from their Iraqi brethren in experience, ranging from the reconciliation between the rivaling Jalal Talabani-led Patriotic Union of Kurdistan party and Masoud Barzani-led Kurdistan Democratic Party, to the gradual, peaceful approach to achieving autonomy within a nation state should the effort to attain full integration fail.

In conclusion, it is time for Syria's Kurds to close ranks and join the Syrian people's march for freedom and demand their own basic rights from a future Syrian government, which they themselves must help shape. The Arab revolutions are as historically exceptional and unparalleled as the victory of the Kurd-turned-Arab Saladin over the European Crusaders in the twelfth century, and this time, too, Arabs and the Kurds can join forces to defeat the injustice that has plagued them from within.

SYRIA: THE BATTLEGROUND BETWEEN SUNNIS AND SHIITES

APRIL 11, 2012

In a late 2011 article,[22] I argued that Syria's upheaval thrusts Turkey and Iran into a collision course because they have opposing geostrategic interests in a conflict that neither party can afford to ignore. Four months later, it has become increasingly clear that the Syrian uprising transcends Iran's and Turkey's strategic interests, as it has become the battleground between the Sunni and Shiite communities throughout the Middle East. The Syrian uprising has drawn a clear sectarian line: the Sunni axis, led by Turkey and Saudi Arabia, and the Shiite axis, led by Iran. The new political order that will eventually emerge in Syria will determine not only the ultimate success or failure of Iran's aspiration to become the region's hegemon, but whether or not the Sunni Arab world will maintain its dominance. Hence, the conflict will be long, costly and bloody, reflecting the troubled history between the two sides that has extended over a millennium.

History may not repeat itself but it remains instructive. The Sunni-Shiite schism goes back more than a thousand years, starting with the dispute over the Islamic Caliphate following the death of Prophet Muhammad in 632 CE and carrying through to the conflict between the Shiite Safavid dynasty in Persia and the Sunni Ottoman dynasty in Turkey in the 16th and 17th centuries. This conflict has, in fact, shaped the geography of Shiite Islam to this day: Persia and its periphery are Shiite, and Sunnis are located to its East and West. There were periods of conflict and periods of peace, such as the epoch that existed between the collapse of the Ottoman Empire and the rise of the secular Pahlavi dynasty in Iran in the 1920s. This period was broken by Iran's Islamic revolution in 1979, whose vigorous attempt to export the revolution to its Sunni Arab neighbors and the latter's fierce resistance manifested in the eight-year-long Iran-Iraq war in the 1980s. Given this enduring rivalry, the superficial political effort made by Turkey and Saudi Arabia to obscure the conflict between the Sunnis and Shiites has now been thrown into the spotlight for all to see.

There is no greater evidence of the intense conflict between the Sunnis and the Shiites than the violent clashes in Bahrain where Saudi Arabia directly interfered militarily to quell the Shiite uprising to ensure continued Sunni dominance.[23] However

---

22 See "Keystone Influence: Syria's Arab Spring and the Race For Regional Hegemony," Huffington Post, November 28, 2011, http://www.huffingtonpost.com/alon-benmeir/keystone-influence-syrias_b_1116631.html.

23 Michael Slackman, "The Proxy Battle in Bahrain," *The New York Times*, March 19, 2011, http://www.nytimes.com/2011/03/20/weekinreview/20proxy.html?pagewanted=all&_r=0.

small Bahrain is, it represents a microcosm of the Sunni-Shiite conflict that has engulfed the region. The Sunni insurgency in Iraq continues to terrorize the Shiite majority, resulting in the weekly deaths of dozens of innocent civilians on both sides. The Shiite group Hezbollah in Lebanon continues to support the Syrian government's violent crackdown on its citizens, killing by many estimates nearly 10,000.[24] Sunni Hamas, which has enjoyed financial and military support from Iran while simultaneously receiving political and logistical support from the Syrian Alawite regime (an offshoot of Shiite Islam), has left its headquarters in Damascus and now openly condemns the Syrian Authority's bloodletting against its Sunni population.

Diplomatic tensions rose last week between Ankara and Tehran over statements from Iranian officials about moving the nuclear talks to a more "neutral territory" such as Syria, Iraq, or China, resulting in an angered Turkish Prime Minister Recep Tayyip Erdogan, who bluntly criticized the Iranians' "lack of honesty."[25] A dichotomy on Syria exists between Iran and Turkey: whereas the former supplies the Assad regime with everything it needs, the latter hosts the main opposition body, the Syrian National Council (SNC). This is a reflection of their individual national interests to dominate a country that provides both of them an opportunity to assert themselves as the region's hegemon and attempt to offer a model to the newly-emerging Arab regime to emulate. Above all else, however, the Sunni Islamic movement, just as the ruling Justice and Development Party (AK Party), adamantly opposes Shiite dominance in its neighborhood.

At greater stake in Syria is the national interest of Saudi Arabia as the conservative leader of the Sunni Arab world. A consolidation of Iran's grip over Syria would spread the Shiite influence over the entire crescent of landmass between the Persian Gulf and the Mediterranean. Though Saudi Arabia paid not much heed to Saddam Hussein's ultimate fate (who once threatened to invade the kingdom), handing Iraq to Shiite Iran on a golden platter in the wake of the Iraq war of 2003 was, and remains, deeply troubling to Riyadh. The fact that Iraq is ruled by a Shiite regime closely allied with Tehran explains why Saudi Arabia has provided refuge to Iraq's top Sunni political figure, Vice President Tariq al-Hashimi, whose political conflict with the Shiite Prime Minister al-Maliki resulted in him being sought by Iraqi authorities on terrorism charges.[26] It is critical for

---

24 "Friends of Syria to discuss boosting opposition, helping civilians," *CNN*, March 31, 2012, http://www.cnn.com/2012/03/31/world/meast/syria-unrest.

25 Rick Gladstone, "As Nuclear Talks Near, Iran Softens Criticism of Turkey," *The New York Times*, April 6, 2012. http://www.nytimes.com/2012/04/07/world/middleeast/iran-softens-criticism-of-turkey-as-nuclear-talks-approach.html?_r=1&.

26 Mohammed Jamjoom, "Fugitive Iraqi vice president in Saudi Arabia," *CNN*, April 4, 2012. http://edition.cnn.com/2012/04/04/world/meast/iraq-fugitive-vp/index.html.

Saudi Arabia to pull Syria out of Iran's belly, which explains why the Saudi government is supportive of arming the rebels in Syria in the hope of toppling the Assad regime.

Moreover, there is no love lost between Iran and the Sunni Muslim Brotherhood (MB) – a regional Islamic Sunni movement whose local parties will certainly form the new regimes in Egypt, Libya, and Tunisia. Although all three countries are undergoing a difficult transitional process, they would cheer the collapse of the Assad regime and would do whatever they could to support the emergence of a Sunni government in Syria. The new transitional governments in Libya as well as Tunisia recognize the SNC as the legitimate authority of Syria.[27] Similarly, the turmoil in Egypt did not prevent the MB from clearly indicating that they simply do not see eye to eye with Iran. In fact, the chairman of the Foreign Affairs committee in the Egyptian parliament, the MB's Freedom and Justice Party member Dr. Essam al-Arian, stated ominously that the Arab Spring would also reach Iran.[28]

As international sanctions began to bite and the Iranian leadership began to feel the pain, they agreed to re-engage in negotiations with the P5+1 over their nuclear program. Equally motivating to Tehran, however, is the situation in Syria. The deteriorating conditions in Syria and Iran's nuclear program have become intertwined because Iran's pursuit of nuclear weapons is driven not merely by national security considerations but essentially by Tehran's desire to secure nuclear weapons to bolster its regional hegemony. Assad's Syria is key to this strategy, and its fall would further increase Iran's isolation in a mostly-Sunni neighborhood and cut the direct links between Tehran and its ally Hezbollah in Lebanon. Also, once Assad's Syria is unraveled, the current substantial Iranian influence on Iraqi politics would weaken at a much quicker pace. Indeed, it is more than likely that Iraqi nationalism would eventually trump its internal Sunni-Shiite divide as Iraq historically takes pride in its unique place in Arab culture as the cradle of Arab civilization.

It follows that Iran may well be willing to demonstrate some flexibility in the Istanbul talks on the nuclear issue by using its Russian patrons to convince the West to curb the pressure on Syria to save the Assad regime, and buying time to prevent an attack on their nuclear facilities by Israel and/or the US. From the Iranian perspective, they can always resume the nuclear program at a later date once the Assad regime is re-stabilized and in so doing, can safeguard the Shiite crescent. One can only hope that the West would not fall for the manipulative mastery of the Iranians. Note that

---

27 "Libyan PM 'not aware' of any Syrians training in Libya," *Al Arabiya*, March 8, 2012. http://english.alarabiya.net/articles/2012/03/08/199447.html.

28 Zvi Bar'el, "Muslim Brotherhood lawmaker: Arab Spring headed to Iran," *Haaretz*, February 28, 2012. http://www.haaretz.com/news/middle-east/muslim-brotherhood-lawmaker-arab-spring-headed-to-iran-1.415380.

the sacrifice of a temporary pause in the nuclear program in return for higher political purpose was also tried successfully by Tehran in 2003.[29]

In the wake of the imminent collapse of the Kofi Annan plan to end the conflict in Syria, the leading Sunni countries, Turkey and Saudi Arabia, now have the opportunity and the obligation to bring an end to the Assad regime, halt the massacres, and pave the way for the emergence of a Sunni government in Damascus. To achieve that, both nations (deriving their legitimacy from the Arab League) must provide military assistance to the rebels while Turkey should carve a significant landmass along its border and, along with its NATO allies, enforce a no-fly zone to protect the Syrian refugees and the Free Syrian Army. Moreover, both nations should make every effort to enlist the international community to bestow legitimacy on the SNC to provide the foundation for a transitional government. Such an effort will save Syria as well as the national interest of the Sunni states in the region while depriving Iran of its aspiration to become a regional hegemon potentially equipped with nuclear weapons.

Anything short of that would mean handing Iran a complete victory and surrendering the Middle East to an inevitable, but wider, violent conflict in the future between the two axes of Sunnis and Shiites.

29 James Blitz, "Iran vows not to retreat on nuclear programme," *Financial Times*, November 9, 2011, http://www.ft.com/intl/cms/s/0/57c81dca-0a3d-11e1-92b5-00144feabdc0. html#axzz2ZJke4sSs.

SYRIA'S UNFOLDING TRAGEDY: WHAT CAN BE DONE?

MAY 7, 2012

As the carnage in Syria continues, the powers that are capable of taking serious measures to stop it are busy finding excuses to explain their collective ineptitude. Meanwhile, the Syrian people are paying with their blood day in and day out while the international community is shamelessly hiding behind UN envoy Kofi Annan's plan that was doomed from day one. Since the Syrian government "accepted" the plan a month ago, at least 1,000 Syrians have been killed and thousands more have been displaced.[30] The Arab League (AL), the United States, the European Union, and Turkey, who in particular can collectively stop Assad's killing machine, still pin their hopes on a plan that Assad has, with impunity, already turned into yet another mockery of the international community.

For obvious reasons, Kofi Annan would like to believe that his plan can still work, but this wishful thinking is like trying to resuscitate a dead man. His insistence on giving the plan more time does nothing but play into Assad's hands. Meanwhile, the death toll is mounting and inaction is preventing other potentially more viable options from being tested. All scenarios of Annan's plan are leading to failure. As the previous (and futile) AL observer mission indicated, Assad is repeating the practice he has excelled at thus far – stopping the aggression against peaceful demonstrators when the observers are around and resuming the killing once they have left. In a country like Syria that comprises an area of 185,000 square kilometers and is populated by 23 million people,[31] this tactic could easily be maintained even if the number of UN observers is increased ten-fold to the 300 observers that France desires.[32]

At the same time, Assad's clique shrewdly realizes the limitations and constraints of an international military intervention. Assad knows that in the midst of presidential elections, and having just concluded one war in Iraq and still fighting another in Afghanistan, the United States will not risk military intervention in another Middle East conflict unless large-scale massacres are committed. For that reason, the Assad regime is regulating how many people should be killed per day, a number that varies between 50 and 100, in

---

30 Neil MacFarquhar, "Cease-Fire in Syria Exposes Heavy Price of Just Buying Time," *The New York Times*, April 28, 2012. http://www.nytimes.com/2012/04/29/world/middleeast/cease-fire-in-syria-buying-time-at-a-cost.html.

31 "Syria."

32 "France warns of UN resolution on use of force in Syria," *France 24*, April 26, 2012. http://www.france24.com/en/20120425-syria-juppe-united-nations-observers-france-chapter-7-resolution-observers-troops-peacekeeping.

order not to trigger an intervention.[33] Moreover, he understands that no Arab country has the military muscle or the will to intervene militarily, including Egypt, which in any case is marred in its own turmoil. Assad has further calculated that the fractured nature of the Syrian opposition makes it unlikely for the AL and the international community to arm the rebels, out of concern that Syria will be torn apart and fall into a prolonged al-Qaeda-led sectarian conflict that might well spread to Lebanon, Turkey, Jordan, or Iraq. Alas, his calculations seem to be working as he continues to defy the international community with impunity. In the midst of all the ongoing slaughter, Assad is proceeding with parliamentary elections, adding insult to the national injury.

For these reasons, other options must be explored, provided they are executed in concert to have a greater and more immediate effect. Iraq can provide a basis for changing the dynamic, especially because Baghdad has a vested interest in stabilizing its own neighborhood. Due to a confluence of unique circumstances, including holding the presidency of the AL, retaining the ability to provide vast material resources, occupying a unique geostrategic position between Syria and Iran, hosting the upcoming talks on Iran's nuclear program, and filling the absence of Egyptian or Saudi leadership while enjoying a greater influence on the Assad regime than any other Arab country, Iraq can play a pivotal role in diffusing the crisis in Syria.

Finally, the Arab states should remember that Iraq has a strong desire to return to the Arab fold and be embraced by it. Indeed, Iraq's Arab nationalism will trump its sectarian divide and its present Shiite affinity to Iran. For these reasons, Iraq should be encouraged to play a role that no other state within the AL can currently perform. The Arab states should also bear in mind that the greater and faster the integration of Iraq back into the Arab fold, the greater the distance will be created between Iraq and Syria from Iran.

Iraq, as president of the AL, can call for new summit meetings and introduce a resolution that offers safe passage and refuge for Assad and his cohorts. In so doing, the Syrian people would look to Iraq as a positive neighbor, rather than one that allowed the sectarian conflict to continue unabated. If the AL officially endorsed such a plan, it could provide at least a plausible opportunity for Assad to consider, although perhaps not immediately. But even under the most far-fetched, ideal scenario where Assad faithfully abides by the cease-fire and creates a space for non-violent protests to re-emerge, there is still no way out. The shooting of peaceful demonstrators that killed four students at Aleppo University strongly suggests that the Assad regime has no intention of allowing peaceful demonstrations as required by Annan's plan. Assad and his lieutenants recognize that however peaceful future protests may be, the protesters

33 Akil Hashem, "Former Syrian General Akil Hashem on the Uprising in Syria," *Foreign Affairs*, April 16, 2012. http://www.foreignaffairs.com/print/134659.

will still demand, along with political reforms, accountability for the thousands of Syrian people killed and tortured by Assad's forces. If justice is not served, revenge killings will be extracted. They further know that there is already bad blood and will have to fight to the finish simply because they are fighting for their own lives, which at one point in the near future may make safe passage an attractive option.

Assad will not choose this option at this juncture unless mounting pressure is brought to bear on his regime. This is where the US can make a significant difference. Frustrated with the Annan plan but constrained by a presidential election, President Obama is more than likely to rule out any direct military intervention. That said, the US still has a responsibility to ratchet up the pressure by resorting to truly crippling sanctions and encouraging others (in particular the European Union and the Arab states) to act accordingly. The current sanctions, including a ban on overseas travel by Syrian senior government officials,34 are important but not effective enough to have a real impact. Instead, strict financial sanctions should target Assad and his government and military leaders. In addition to the Central Bank of Syria, the US should target the commercial Bank of Syria and other financial institutions while continuing to provide the opposition with communications gear and much-needed intelligence, logistical support, and medical and other non-lethal equipment.

Russia and China, which have earlier vetoed UN Security Council resolutions on Syria, may now change their positions. Vladimir Putin, who has just assumed the presidency, might have good reason to shift Russia's policy toward the Assad regime. Frustrated with Assad's devious maneuverings, increasingly concerned over Russia's standing in the eyes of the Arab world, and coupled with his personal ambitions to appear as the peacemaker, Putin might move to sacrifice Assad while still preserving Russia's strategic interest in Syria. That is why the US must now explore this possibility while encouraging the Syrian National Council (SNC) to reach an understanding with Moscow, according to which the latter's strategic interest in the "new Syria," especially Russia's naval base in the Syrian Mediterranean port of Tartous, would be respected. In return, Russia would show its support of a new UN Security Council resolution that would condemn the Assad regime and call for his departure. China, revealing that it is already wavering as it has called on the Syrian government to respond to Annan's plan35 and is expressing deep concerns over the continuation of violence, may well follow suit.

---

34 "Updated: A Guide to Sanctions on Syria," *Frontline*, November 30, 2011, http://www.pbs.org/wgbh/pages/frontline/foreign-affairs-defense/syria-undercover/a-guide-to-sanctions-on-syria/.

35 "China calls on Syria to implement peace plan," *The Daily Star*, April 11, 2012. http://www.dailystar.com.lb/News/Middle-East/2012/Apr-11/169884-china-calls-on-syria-to-implement-peace-plan.ashx#axzz1tqXD3C44.

Should all of these efforts fail, it will then be absolutely critical to resort to the Benghazi solution. What is crucial here is the idea of carving out a sizeable portion of Syrian territory along the Turkish border to serve as a safe haven for refugees and offering a base for the military defectors to re-group and launch military operations against Assad's forces. To this end, Turkey is a central player. Ankara is extremely concerned over the deteriorating conditions in Syria. With the moral and semi-legal support of the AL and with logistical support from the EU and the US, Turkey might well come to the conclusion that this last option would entail considerably less risks than allowing the situation to unfold into uncontrollable chaos. The aim is to impose a no-fly zone over northern Syria, bordering Turkey. No air strikes should be conducted against Syrian targets unless the Syrian air force threatens the protected "Free Syria" zone. The SNC would be based in this zone, creating a new governing authority and preparing to take over as a transitional government.

There is no easy solution to the Syrian debacle and the Annan plan has now become an obstacle rather than a plan that provides a solution to the conflict. Short of exploring these options immediately, a full scale civil war will certainly erupt, leaving trails of blood behind while the international community continues to shamelessly hide behind Kofi Annan's plan that was dead on arrival.

SYRIA: THE INTERNATIONAL TRAVESTY

JUNE 25, 2012

After fifteen months of relentless slaughter, the developments in Syria, with shockingly inordinate amounts of slain women and children, have demonstrated the international community's ineptitude and contemptible moral bankruptcy in the face of horrific carnage. The failure to stop the crisis stems from the international community's unwillingness to take stern measures to end the killing while it continues to take cover under the Annan plan and mouths countless verbal condemnations of the Assad regime, knowing full well that they will not succeed. Those that can change the course of events in Syria, including the US, EU, Turkey, and the Arab League, have shamefully demonstrated the most startling shortsightedness coupled with wishful thinking in the face of insurmountable odds.

With the suspension of the observer mission in Syria,36 Mr. Annan has conjured yet another "ingenious" reformation of his beleaguered plan by calling for the creation of a "Syria Contact Group"37 that perplexingly includes Iran and Russia, who have and continue to provide President Assad with the means by which he slaughters his own people. While Mr. Annan is genuinely trying to end the killings by diplomatic means, his desire to preserve his reputation as an international mediator continues to stand in the way. Annan's new plan (like the previous ones) will soon prove futile. Meanwhile, thousands of more innocent Syrians will die due to the West's inability to garner the moral courage to decisively act.

In scenes of grotesque horror, thousands of children have been killed since Syria's uprising began, and thousands more have suffered unimaginable torture and abuse.38 With utter depravity, fathers have been forced to witness the mutilation and execution of their young children, only to soon meet the same fate as that of their family members.[39] Young girls and women suffer the wickedness of sexual violence at the hands of unconscionable monsters and are then killed in full view of

---

36 Peter S. Green, "Syria Observer Mission to Remain Suspended, UN Says," *Bloomberg*, June 19, 2012, http://www.bloomberg.com/news/2012-06-19/syria-observer-mission-to-remain-suspended-un-says.html.

37 Louis Charbonneau, "Annan floats idea to rescue failing Syria peace plan-envoys," *Reuters*, June 6, 2012. http://www.reuters.com/article/2012/06/06/us-syria-un-idUSBRE85513220120606.

38 "UNICEF steps up its response to children affected by the crisis in Syria," *UNICEF*, March 23, 2012. http://www.unicef.org/media/media_62075.html.

39 Richard Spencer and Ruth Sherlock, "Massacred Syrian children were 'bound before being shot'," *The Telegraph*, May 28, 2012. http://www.telegraph.co.uk/news/worldnews/middleeast/syria/9295268/Massacred-Syrian-children-were-bound-before-being-shot.html.

their loved ones.[40] Though barely scratching the surface, these events stand in stark contrast to the machinations of the international community, specifically those powers who can feasibly act to end the suffering. Whether out of their unique political interests in sustaining the Assad regime (i.e. Russia, China, and Iran) or the weak lack of will and misguided political calculations by Western powers to intervene, there is no willingness to provide the opposition with the necessary equipment to effectively defend themselves and absolutely no appetite to use military means against the government's merciless onslaught.

To top this inexcusable display, the support for the first Annan plan that passed the United Nations Security Council precisely due to its toothless character set the lowest denominator possible for international action. Prior to the resolution that adopted Annan's initiative, Russia and China were responsible for blocking the Arab League-backed effort in the Security Council that called on Assad to cede power and begin a political transition,[41] thereby jettisoning any hope for a political solution to the conflict. The formation of a contact group at this juncture is ill-conceived and will prove as hopelessly ineffective as the first Annan plan. This course of action will no doubt provide Assad with more time to continue slaughtering his citizens unabated.

The confounding irony of the contact group proposal is the call for Iranian participation,[42] which defies all logic given Iran's role in providing crucial support to Assad's regime in the form of men and material, which has enabled the Assad government to continue its unconscionable conduct. Whereas Russia's involvement may be deemed necessary by virtue of its deep relations with and influence on Assad, Iran is complicit in the day-to-day massacres in a desperate effort to maintain the Alawite (a sect that has roots in Shia Islam) domination.[43] Iran represents a country that has been destabilizing the Middle East since its own revolution in 1979, a country that has been behind the insurgency in Iraq for the past decade,[44] a country that is racing toward the development of a nuclear weapon, a country that has defied five Security Council resolutions while preventing the International Atomic Energy Agency

40 Sima Barmania, "Women under siege: The use of rape as a weapon of war in Syria," *The Independent,* June 19, 2012. http://blogs.independent.co.uk/2012/06/19/women-under-siege-the-use-of-rape-as-a-weapon-of-war-in-syria/.

41 Louis Charbonneau and Patrick Worsnip, "Russia, China veto U.N. draft backing Arab plan for Syria," *Reuters,* February 4, 2012. http://www.reuters.com/article/2012/02/04/us-syria-idUSTRE80S08620120204.

42 Nayla Razzouk and Indira A.R. Lakshmanan, "UN's Annan Says Iran Should Help to End Conflict in Syria," *Bloomberg,* June 22, 2012. http://www.bloomberg.com/news/2012-06-22/un-s-annan-says-iran-should-help-to-end-conflict-in-syria.html.

43 "The 'secretive sect' in charge of Syria," *BBC News,* May 17, 2012. http://www.bbc.co.uk/news/world-middle-east-18084964.

44 Lionel Beehner and Greg Bruno, "Iran's Involvement in Syria," *Council on Foreign Relations,* March 3, 2008. http://www.cfr.org/iran/irans-involvement-iraq/p12521#p2.

(IAEA) from conducting unrestricted inspections, a country under intense international sanctions due to its intransigence, and a country that seeks regional hegemony by preserving, at all costs, the "Shia Crescent" that stretches from the Persian Gulf to the Mediterranean.45 Mr. Annan's wisdom leads him to believe that Iran should be part of the solution when in fact it is very much a part of the problem. In light of Iran's aforementioned record, his supposed wisdom bears no further comment.

Suppose an international contact group is formed with or without Iran. By what measure and means will it succeed if the intention is merely to remove Assad from power? Even if Assad is replaced with a liberal reformer who dedicates himself to human rights and equality, there is no chance for success when the entire government apparatus (thousands of individuals from the internal security, military, intelligence services, the interior ministry, as well as the Ba'ath elite, who have vested interests in maintaining the current order and fighting for their lives) remains in place. In supporting Annan's new proposal, the international community is engaging in an illusory approach that is guaranteed to fail at the expense of the very lives of the Syrian people. It is extremely difficult not to conjure up a higher form of hypocrisy and ineptitude.

Though the conflict is spiraling into a civil war,[46] there are two potential options to solve the crisis. The first is to offer Assad immunity from criminal prosecution and provide him, his family and his criminal gang safe passage to a number of Arab countries that are willing to accept them, including Saudi Arabia. This approach presupposes that the removal of Assad will bring about a solution to the conflict, but this claim lacks crucial merit and is ultimately a nonstarter. Indeed, Assad has not merely inherited the Presidency from his father but an entire governing apparatus that has been built around him and stands guilty of these ghastly crimes. Any diplomatic solution that revolves around Assad's exit will have to include the removal of thousands of individuals who lead various branches of the regime. Their departure should be followed by the formation of a coalition that is representative of all Syrian factions and will steer the country through a transitional period of four to five years. The West must avoid the illusion that quick elections will provide a solution—Egypt, Libya, Yemen, and even Tunisia offer glaring examples of the failure of this approach.

Should the undeserved offer of clemency fail, there is no doubt that the Arab League, United States, European Union, and Turkey should join together to decide on military action aimed at bombing selective military targets in Syria. After several sorties, the bombings should stop and a clear message should be sent to Assad that it

45 Ian Black, "Fear of a Shia full moon," *The Guardian*, January 26, 2007, http://www.guardian.co.uk/world/2007/jan/26/worlddispatch.ianblack.
46 Alexander Marquardt and Dana Hughes, "Syria Is in a Civil War, Says UN; Clinton Says Solution Must Be Political," *ABC News*, June 12, 2012. http://abcnews.go.com/blogs/headlines/2012/06/syria-is-in-a-civil-war-says-un-clinton-says-solution-must-be-political/.

would resume unimpeded if he and his clan do not relinquish their positions. Although I prefer a peaceful solution, in times of tragic impasse, it takes a certain level of counter-violence to prevent a much greater catastrophe. Now that a Turkish jet fighter has been shot down by Syrian air defense, and if NATO stands firmly behind Turkey, Ankara will likely be more inclined to carve out a large section of Syria to provide cover and space from which Syrian opposition forces can operate while providing aid to refugees and protecting the whole area by imposing a no-fly zone. Russia, Iran, or China will not risk challenging the US and the EU as long as Russia is informed, through private channels, that its interests in Syria will be preserved.

It is time to stop engaging in illusions and shameful hypocrisy and adopt a realistic framework to end the Syrian killing machine. The Alawite-dominated regime has, for decades, subjugated its people to subhuman conditions, denying them basic human rights while letting them be consumed by poverty. The international community must rise up to its moral obligations to halt the bloodshed. The failure to do so will precipitate the loss of credibility of Western powers in the region while submitting to the whims of Russia and Iran and plunge Syria into a full-fledged civil war.

NO RECONCILIATION WITH THE BUTCHER OF DAMASCUS

JULY 16, 2012

I cannot begin this article without first expressing my profound outrage about the behavior of the Western powers, Turkey, the Arab League, and Kofi Annan, all of whom are still debating the likelihood of finding a political solution to end the merciless butchering of the Syrian people by the Assad regime. Do they really think in their heart of hearts that a political solution is possible, given the fact that Assad has defied all previous resolutions while his killing machine continues to erase one Syrian town after another? How ironic it is that the countries that preach the gospel of human rights have resorted to a self-imposed paralysis while justifying it with the presumed lack of legitimacy of intervention. What legitimacy is needed to intervene when thousands of men, women, and children are massacred each month? When does hypocrisy end: when politics trump moral obligation, and when great powers surrender their most precious values to the devil?

I understand the pitfalls and the potentially regional repercussions resulting even from a carefully-planned military intervention. But this must be weighed not only against the systematic butchering of the Syrian people but also against the credibility and the standing of these powers in the eyes of those nations that look up to United States or NATO not to tolerate this kind of travesty, which transcends the cruelest human conduct imagined. What do other despots learn from the Syrian experience and why should they behave any differently toward their own people when they can do so with immunity? For how much longer can those countries that can actually do something to stop the carnage wait? When is enough, enough? How many more Syrians must be killed in cold blood for the consciousness of the international community to be awakened to action? The most recent massacre, estimated to be between 68 and 150 people in the village of Tremseh near the city of Hama,[47] attests not only to Assad's utter ruthlessness but also to his fear that he is about to lose his grip on power. Although Assad has moved some of his chemical weapons either to protect them from falling into the hands of the rebels or as a last-ditch effort to use them against the rebels to save his regime, it will be suicidal as he will be crossing a red line that invites immediate Western military intervention.

---

47 Loveday Morris and Justin Vela, "Assad troops move on Damascus as massacre toll is cut," *The Independent,* July 16, 2012, http://www.independent.co.uk/news/world/middle-east/assad-troops-move-on-damascus-as-massacre-toll-is-cut-7945484.html.

At the time of this writing, the United Nations Security Council (UNSC) will be at it again this Wednesday trying to pass yet another useless and insulting resolution designed to end the conflict peacefully. One would think that by now the United States and NATO members have learned their lessons from previous resolutions that have only allowed Assad to continue the unabated slaughter of his people.

The first draft resolution sponsored by Russia calls for extending the UN observer mission by an additional three months and supports a more political mission by cutting back the number of military observers. In addition, Russia urges both sides to observe a ceasefire, calls for the full implementation of the Annan Plan, and forcefully rejects a Chapter VII mandate which allows for the use of economic and diplomatic sanctions in any and all forms up to, but not including, the use of military force.[48] This resolution is no different from the Annan plan that was dead on arrival and ignored from day one, forcing the UN observers to suspend their mission in the wake of the continuing killings and indiscriminate destruction.

The three Western powers (the US, Britain and France) drafted a more forceful resolution that would give Assad ten days to comply with the full implementation of the Annan plan by first withdrawing troops from populated areas. Should he fail to do so, Syria would face diplomatic and economic punishment in addition to the threat of military force under Chapter VII of the UN Charter.[49] Any effort to agree on a compromise between the two resolutions, if successful at all, will end once up again being a toothless resolution that will only give Assad license to continue his massacres without any fear of punishment or serious threats to his regime.

The Western powers might still offer their resolution for a vote through the UNSC even though they expect Russia to exercise its veto power. The advantage they would reap from such an exercise is to paint Russia as a complicit party to the abhorrent developments in Syria, which are sliding the state quickly toward full-fledged civil war, as the Red Cross has already characterized the bloodshed.[50] Although Russia's position would be greatly undermined in the eyes of the Arab states, the mass killings would continue.

The outcry of the Syrian people has been heard time and time again but the international community remains paralyzed, engaged in wishful thinking that somehow the Assad regime will heed their call. This obviously will not happen, and now Western

48 Edith M. Lederer, "Europe, Russia propose rival resolutions on Syria," Associated Press, April 20, 2012, http://news.yahoo.com/europe-russia-propose-rival-resolutions-syria-182901110.html.
49 "U.N. chief doubts Assad's peace pledge; Annan says Syria flouted resolutions," *Al Arabiya News*, July 13, 2012, http://www.alarabiya.net/articles/2012/07/13/226209.html.
50 Neil MacFarquhar, "Syria Denies Attack on Civilians, in Crisis Seen as Civil War," *The New York Times*, July 15, 2012, http://www.nytimes.com/2012/07/16/world/middleeast/syria-denies-use-of-heavy-weapons-in-deadly-village-fight.html.

powers, along with Turkey, must muster the courage and decide on a course of action that will bring an end to a regime that has long since lost any remaining vestiges of humanity. Assad and his cronies must go. Under no circumstances can there be any reconciliation between the butcher of Damascus and the international community or Syria's people.

The time has come for a coordinated military intervention with or without Russian consent. A safe haven must be established in the north and south of the country, spearheaded by Turkey with the support of NATO. A no-fly zone should go into effect immediately, medical, financial, and military aid should be provided to the opposition forces, and selected Syrian military targets should be bombed. Simultaneously, a clear message should be sent to Assad that the bombings will escalate until he steps down from power. The West, along with the Arab League, should offer him and the hundreds of culprits from his military, police, and intelligence services safe passage to a third country, provided he makes the decision to leave within two weeks and on the condition that he immediately stop the slaughter of his people. In so doing, the US, unlike Russia, could increase its leverage with the Syrians once Assad is deposed.

The concern that such a military intervention may plunge the Middle East into regional conflict is baseless. The last thing that Assad would venture to do is to challenge Turkey and its NATO allies. Moreover, to draw Israel into the conflict would invite counterattacks that could obliterate his power base. Iran, which is under tremendous international pressure because of its defiance of the international community in connection with its nuclear program, will think twice before it directly interferes, fearing that this may provide the United States or Israel the pretext to attack its nuclear installations. Hezbollah will seek to preserve its position and is unlikely to come to Assad's aid, knowing full-well that the Assad regime has run its course.

Finally, Russia can do nothing to prevent Western and Turkish interference with the support of the Arab League other than condemning their actions. Moreover, Russia knows that for all intents and purposes the Assad regime is finished. It is not unlikely that if Russia also knows of the inevitable Western military intervention, it may decide to make a deal with the West and Turkey with the blessing of the Arab League and the Syrian opposition (as was recently discussed between the opposition and Russia) to ensure its strategic interests in the region and sacrifice the Assad regime in return. As I have stated time and again, such a course of action will provide the West a momentous opportunity to extract Syria out of Iran's belly which might force Iran to rethink its regional strategy as well as its nuclear ambition.

Time is running out. The longer Western powers wait, the more Syrians will die on the altar of international ineptitude. There are no excuses left for the West to hide behind its contrived political calculations and lose what is left of its moral standing.

THE SYRIAN CRISIS: PITTING RUSSIA AGAINST THE U.S.

JULY 30, 2012

The latest UN resolution sponsored by the Western powers (the United States, England and France), designed to increase the pressure on Assad and force him to step down, was once again rejected by Russia and China,[51] making it abundantly clear that all diplomatic efforts have come to a dead end. If Russia, the main proponent of the Assad regime (and the country that vetoed three consecutive UN resolutions to force Assad's hand) still believes that Assad can survive and will support him to the bitter end, Moscow is making a colossal mistake. Conversely, if the United States continues to issue one toothless condemnation after another and seeks cover under hollow political plans to oust Assad, it will end up in no better position than Russia. The truth is that neither Russia nor the United States believes that the Assad regime can survive. Thus, they must now agree on a way to find a solution that rests on coercive diplomacy acceptable to both while preserving their interests.

Indeed, there are many irrefutable facts that strongly suggest Assad is doomed. The ongoing violence is escalating and gradually tipping the scales in favor of the rebels. The remarkable success of the Syrian rebels who killed four top officials in charge of executing Assad's brutal crackdown has dramatically increased the level of uncertainty and demoralized many of Assad's top commanders.[52] The number of defectors, top officials including the Syrian ambassador to Iraq, Nawaf al-Fares and Brigadier General Manaf Tlas, has burgeoned and it is becoming increasingly more difficult for Assad to find individuals he can trust from his ever-shrinking pool of loyalists. Emboldened by their successes in attacking Assad's power base, the rebels have made great strides in their ability to organize and plan ways of inflicting ever greater casualties on his better-trained and better-equipped regular army and militia forces. Finally, the failures of all diplomatic efforts have forced Western powers, along with Turkey and the Arab League (AL), to seek alternate solutions outside the United Nations Security Council (UNSC) by funneling greater supplies and more sophisticated weaponry, communications gear, intelligence, and other necessary provisions to rebel forces. Regardless of how important these measures are in aiding the rebels, they unfortunately remain insufficient to dramatically tip the balance in favor of the opposition and ensure the speedy demise of the Assad regime.

---

51 Michelle Nichols, "Russia, China veto U.N. Security Council resolution on Syria," *Reuters*, July 19, 2012. http://www.reuters.com/article/2012/07/19/us-syria-crisis-un-idUSBRE86I0UD20120719.

52 Black.

Although all of those reasons (and others) make it impossible for Assad to survive, Russia's President Putin is not so naïve as to think that the Syrian upheaval is an aberration and is likely cognizant that it is part and parcel of the Arab Spring. The uprising of Arab youth in Syria who have witnessed the demise of Egypt's Mubarak, Libya's Qaddafi, Yemen's Saleh, and Tunisia's Ben Ali are no longer willing to live in subjugation, humiliation and hopelessness. There is no political framework, regardless of its framers, that will succeed unless it meets their aspirations. Putin knows that regardless of how many more weapons he supplies Assad with and how much longer he can delay the inevitable, in the end the Assad regime is doomed.

Concerned over his deteriorating domestic position, Putin, who is now seen as complicit to the slaughter, will seek to contain the damage sooner rather than later as the Kremlin is certainly guided by Russia's greater interests in the region. President Obama also understands that the US will further lose much of its remaining credibility and influence if it continues to take cover under abortive diplomatic efforts and engage in empty rhetoric hopelessly aimed at ending the conflict (notwithstanding the re-election campaign) when hundreds of Syrians are killed daily. Indeed, the reluctance to allow for outside interference to the unfolding crisis will bring the crisis to the doorsteps of both Russia and the US.

It is clear that Russia will seek to protect its interests in the Middle East, and views the deteriorating crisis in Damascus with alarm knowing that sticking to its current policy is self-defeating. It is clear that the US also has major stakes in the region and the unfolding events in Syria could seriously undermine the US' overall strategic interest. Although the US, by virtue of its extensive Middle East alliances, has the upper hand, Russia can still prevent the US and its allies from having it their way as has clearly been demonstrated thus far.

Russia, however, also knows that without collaborating with the US on the future of Syria, Moscow will have little say in shaping or influencing the eventual new political order that will emerge from the ashes of a prolonged violence and chaos replete with revenge and retribution, and from which the Islamists will benefit the most. Therefore, the time has come for the two powers, in partnership with the Syrian National Council (SNC), the AL, and Turkey, to fully collaborate in the search for an outcome that will preserve much of their respective interests while simultaneously preventing the crisis from "spinning out of control," as Secretary of Defense Panetta recently proclaimed.[53] Indeed, neither Russia nor the US (albeit both approaching the conflict from different angles) can allow the crisis to destroy the country through tens of thousands of casualties without severely undercutting their immediate and long-term interests.

---

53 Luis Ramirez, "Panetta: Syrian Violence 'Spinning Out of Control,'" *Voice of America*, July 18, 2012. http://www.voanews.com/content/panetta_syrian_violence_spinning_out_of_control/1419092.html.

It should be noted that on more than one occasion, Russia's Foreign Minister Sergei Lavrov has stated that Russia is not wedded to President Assad and would not object to a solution to end the crisis under unspecified circumstances.[54] The prospect, if not the certainty of a full-fledged civil war (the Red Cross has already declared the crisis as such),[55] may now have created the circumstances for the US and Russia to forge a strategy to force Assad out by supporting the SNC's efforts toward the same objective. As stated above, Putin knows that continuing to support Assad to the bitter end is a losing proposition and losing Syria will be a major blow to Russia's overall strategic interests in the region. If Putin can strike a deal with the US and the SNC that preserves Russia's interests in Syria and negotiates with the US on bilateral issues of critical importance to Russia, Putin may well be prepared to sacrifice Assad. Once Assad, through private Russian channels, is told that he is about to lose Moscow's support, he may then opt for a safe passage to another country and avoid Qaddafi's fate.

Should Assad refuse to heed the Russian call, to save face Russia could then openly express its concerns that the crisis in Syria is indeed spinning out of control and endangering the region's stability. To that end, Russia would be prepared to sponsor a UNSC resolution on behalf of the AL under Chapter VII that authorizes the imposition of sanctions and the *potential* use of force should Assad refuse to relinquish power. The resolution should also authorize the supply of military equipment to stop tanks and jet fighters, provide logistical assistance to the opposition, and allow the rebels to hold on to a large swath of territory in the north and south. This will provide sanctuary for the expected massive increase of refugees and establish an area for the Syrian Free Army to stage major operations against the regime. To that end, the US and Russia would then help the SNC to organize and present a unified agenda that incorporates all social groups and religious sects in Syria, particularly the Kurdish, Christian, and the Alawite minorities. The collaboration of necessity between Russia and the US will avoid a horrific outcome from which both countries will suffer a humiliating setback.

It is imperative that the SNC is prepared to take over the government apparatus when Assad leaves by establishing a shadow government comprised of figures that must include some of those that have recently escaped from Syria. Once the SNC presents a united front, the support it receives from the West (and Russia) should be conditional upon a longer transitional period of three to five years before elections take place. In this manner, new (secular) political parties will have a much better chance to organize and prepare comprehensive political platforms

54 Miriam Elder, "Syria massacre: opposition forces share blame, says Russian minister," *The Guardian*, May 28, 2012, http://www.guardian.co.uk/world/2012/may/28/syria-massacre-opposition-shares-blame-russian.
55 MacFarquhar.

while substantially reducing the chances of the Islamists to capture power, which neither Russia, the US, nor the SNC wants.

In addition, the US and Russia should be prepared to sponsor a second UN resolution that would authorize the establishment of a peacekeeping force, ideally comprised of a minimum of 10-15,000 soldiers from Arab States. Preferably, this force should fall under the joint command of Saudi Arabia and Egypt with external advisers from the West and Russia to provide logistical and technical support. Such a force must have the mandate to take action to maintain peace if necessary in order for it to operate effectively within Syria.

Considering the multiple conflicting issues between all of the players whose interests will be affected by the outcome of the crisis in Syria, this approach may well be seen as far-fetched. But by leaving the crisis to take its own course, everyone will end up a loser and the Middle East will be plunged into a horrifyingly unpredictable future.

ALON BEN-MEIR

IRAN'S INTERVENTION IN SYRIA MUST BE STOPPED

AUGUST 9, 2012

As the situation in Syria continues to deteriorate with the collapse of the Assad regime becoming increasingly more imminent, further direct intervention by Iran in the Syrian conflict in an effort to save the regime should not be ruled out. For Iran, the Assad regime represents the linchpin to their regional hegemonic ambitions and as such, preserving the regime is central to safeguarding Tehran's axis of influence, which encompasses Syria, Iraq, and Lebanon.[56] Direct Iranian involvement in Syria, while a given, further aggravates the already volatile situation in the Middle East. The question is: when will the Western powers led by the US, the Arab states, Turkey, and Israel take the necessary and credible steps to force Tehran to stop meddling in Syria's internal affairs and prevent it from playing a direct role in an effort to quell the Syrian uprising?

Having already sent military advisers along with members of Iran's Revolutionary Guards disguised as pilgrims, and pledging firm support for the Syrian government,[57] it is hard to imagine that, left to its own devices, Tehran will stay idle in the face of Assad's imminent demise. Should Iran decide to further deepen its involvement in Syria, it would be based on long-term considerations rather than an aim to achieve an immediate advantage. Indeed, from the Iranian perspective, regardless of how the crisis in Syria may unfold, Tehran is determined to maintain its influence, as the loss of Syria would represent a colossal defeat and severely weaken Iran's hold on the "Shiite Crescent," which extends from the Persian Gulf to the Mediterranean. Thus, Tehran may conclude that however risky its involvement may be, without taking such risks it will not only be marginalized in Syria but could ultimately doom its ambitions to remain a significant regional contender, if not the region's hegemon.

Whereas until recently Iran tried to obscure its involvement in Syria, in the past few days Iranian lawmakers called on their government to tell the Iranian public why Syria under Assad is of strategic importance. Ahmad Reza Dastgheib, Deputy Head of Iran's Majlis Committee of National Security and Foreign Policy, said: "We should make all our efforts to prevent the Syrian government from falling."[58] In a further indication of Iran's concerns over the future of the Assad regime, it has dispatched high

---

56 Joanna Paraszczuk, "Iranian lawmaker pushes for Syria transparency," *The Jerusalem Post*, August 7, 2012. http://www.jpost.com/MiddleEast/Article.aspx?id=280334.

57 "Iran pledges support as Syria fighting rages," *Al Jazeera*, August 7, 2012. http://www.aljazeera.com/news/middleeast/2012/08/201287142241794676.html.

58 Paraszczuk.

level officials including Saeed Jalili, the head of Iran's Supreme National Security Council, to assure Assad that Iran will not allow its close partnership with the Syrian leadership to be shaken by the uprising or external foes. Jalili further emphasized that Tehran will do everything in its power to help him effectively deal with the foreign elements that seek the collapse of the regime.[59] Whether driven by deep convictions or wishful thinking, many Iranians still believe that the prospect of Assad's survival remains strong and that with continuing assistance, Assad will prevail while Iran safeguards its interests and still emerges as a nuclear power.

This posturing, buttressed by real military and economic assistance, may well be the forerunner of a greater, more transparent and direct involvement of Iran in the Syrian crisis. Tehran is not convinced, as of yet, that the Western powers (led by the United States) will in fact challenge Iran directly should Iran decide to play a more direct and active role to save both the Assad regime and their larger regional interests. Iran knows that the Western powers and Israel, along with Turkey and the Arab states, would like to pull Syria outside of Iran's orbit. To persuade Iran that its continuing involvement in Syria is short-lived, the US, the Arab League (AL), the EU, and Turkey must work in concert and adopt coercive, oriented measures to demonstrate to the Iranian Mullahs that this is a no-win situation and that their continued involvement could be disastrous for the regime.

The Arab states' reaction must not be limited to another declaration of outrage as previously expressed by the AL.[60] While the AL might refrain from attacking Iranian forces outright, countries such as Saudi Arabia and Qatar should openly expand their supply of military equipment, financial aid, medical supplies and other necessary provisions to the Syrian opposition in order to shift the conflict to the rebels' advantage. That said, any step taken by the AL short of military action, which in any case is untenable, will not necessarily change the power equation in Syria as Assad will mercilessly use any military means available to him to stay in power. But transparent Arab support will send a clear message to Iran that its involvement in Syria may cost Tehran more than it is willing to pay.

Israel, who would certainly feel directly threatened by an Iranian presence in a neighboring country, should also send a clear warning to Iran, if it has not already: Israel will not hesitate to take any action deemed necessary to protect its national security interests. The implications of the Israeli threat may well be fully understood in Tehran and regardless of how much the Iranian regime boasts about its military prowess, it will no doubt think twice before it fully commits to salvaging Syria with

59 Farnaz Fassihi, "Tensions Rise Over Iranian Hostages," *The Wall Street Journal*, August 8, 2012, http://online.wsj.com/article/SB10000872396390443792604577575221903873222.html.
60 "Arab League urges Syria to 'stop bloodshed'," *Al Jazeera*, September 14, 2011. http://www.aljazeera.com/news/middleeast/2011/09/201191314579931618.html.

such costs. Iran also understands that should it end up being present on Israel's borders, Israel would be provided with an excuse to attack Iranian nuclear facilities. Of particular concern to Israel are Syria's chemical and biological weapons, which may fall into the hands of militant Islamist groups who may seek to attack Israel at the first opportune moment.[61] Israel should also warn Iran that Israel will hold their leaders responsible for any such provocation and that Iran will suffer horrific consequences.

As I have stated before,[62] Syria has become a battleground between the Shiite and Sunni communities. The involvement of Shiite Iran in Syria would assuredly change Turkey's (which is predominantly Sunni) position altogether. Notwithstanding the ongoing discussion between Ankara and Tehran, Turkey should make it abundantly clear that Iran's direct interference in Syria will not occur with impunity. Regardless of the existing strategic military alliance between Iran and Syria, this does not provide Iran with a license to intervene, particularly because Syria is not threatened by outside powers. Such Iranian interference should prompt Turkey to carve a large swath of land that connects Aleppo with Turkey in which a safe haven for Syrian refugees and an operational base for the Syrian Free Army would be established while, with the support of Western powers, a no-fly zone over the seized Syrian territory would be imposed.

Russia, who has been adamantly against outside interference, will certainly continue to support Iran tacitly but can do little to prevent the countries concerned from acting against Iran should Tehran's involvement become increasingly more transparent. Notwithstanding the fact that Russia would like to maintain Iran's influence in Syria, currently and in the post-Assad era, Moscow's interest would, at a minimum, be served by working with the United States to prevent Syria's biological and chemical weapons from falling into the wrong hands.

Finally, and most importantly, having been augmenting its naval forces in the Persian Gulf as part of its preparations to stop Iran from acquiring nuclear weapons and having been morally emboldened by the United Nations General Assembly's resolution (passed with an overwhelming majority) condemning Assad's atrocities, the US poses the greatest threat to Iran. For this reason, Iran is not likely to defy the American warnings, as stated by Secretary of State Hillary Clinton, that the US will not tolerate any power to cross such a red line.[63] For Iran to take the American warning seriously, the United States'

---

61 Nicholas Blanford, "Syria's chemical weapons: How secure are they?," *The Christian Science Monitor*, June 26, 2012. http://www.csmonitor.com/World/Middle-East/2012/0626/Syria-s-chemical-weapons-How-secure-are-they.

62 See "Syria: The Battleground Between Sunnis and Shiites," page 103.

63 Peter Baker and Michael R. Gordon, "U.S. Warns Syria on Chemical Weapons," *The New York Times*, December 3, 2012, http://www.nytimes.com/2012/12/04/world/middleeast/nato-prepares-missile-defenses-for-turkey.html.

warning must not be veiled by political ambiguities, as Iran will not be deterred from aiding Assad militarily unless the threat to them is clear and credible. To that end, the US must take decisive measures without necessarily placing military boots on Syrian territory.

In this regard, the US should move from debating the need for imposing a no-fly zone to implementing it with the support of Turkey and work with other countries, including Russia, and the rebels to safeguard Syria's stockpile of chemical weapons. Moreover, the US must facilitate the supply of anti-tank and anti-aircraft weapons, and encourage top Syrian officials to defect now with the promise of having a future in the new Syrian government. The US must also make it abundantly clear to the Syrian National Council and the Syrian Free Army that they must work in concert and send a warning to all Syrian minorities that they have a serious stake in Syria's future and only if they work together will they will blunt further Iranian interference and ensure peaceful transition instead of plunging into sectarian war that will tear Syria apart. Short of taking these measures, the United States will risk the opportunity not only to remove Syria from Iran's belly but also forsake the chance of playing a significant role in shaping the new political order in Syria.

The ultimate question is: will Iran gamble by taking such a risk? The answer, I believe, rests with Tehran's paramount desire to preserve first and foremost its own regime, and that may well depend on whether or not Tehran takes the threats of Western and regional powers seriously. This is the time when only action matters. Otherwise, the region will be swept into a horrifying conflagration in which every state will be a loser, especially the United States and its allies.

PALESTINE

PALESTINE

TURKEY: RECONCILING BETWEEN ISRAEL AND HAMAS

JANUARY 16, 2012

While the representatives of Israel, the Palestinian Authority and the Quartet (the US, EU, Russia, and the UN) were recently hosted in Amman, Jordan, in an effort to revive the Israeli-Palestinian peace process, Turkey's Prime Minister Erdogan met in Ankara with Hamas' Prime Minister, Ismail Haniyeh, who remains openly committed to Israel's destruction and opposes any peace negotiations with Israel.[1] This does not suggest that Mr. Erdogan's support of Hamas' position is against Israeli-Palestinian peace, but this raises the question as to whether or not Mr. Erdogan is willing to play a constructive role in mitigating the Israel-Hamas discord or whether he will continue to shore up Hamas' obstructionist position to the detriment of Israeli-Palestinian peace.

For Turkey to play a leading and constructive regional role, especially in the Israeli-Palestinian peace process, it needs first to regain its credibility with Israel. The prudent thing for the Turkish Prime Minister to do is to openly balance his tenacious demands of Israel to modify its position toward Hamas, for example, by putting an end to the blockade in Gaza. Similarly, he should equally demand that Hamas' leadership change their posture by accepting Israel's right to exist and renouncing violent resistance as the means by which to achieve a solution to the Israeli-Palestinian conflict.

Erdogan's open-ended support of Hamas, which is mainly rooted in his Islamic affinity to the organization (as many observers suspect of being the case), places the Turkish Prime Minister in a position to persuade Hamas' leadership to permanently abandon violence and accept a two-state solution through peaceful negotiations for its own sake. Indeed, however indispensable Hamas may be to a permanent and secure Israeli-Palestinian peace, as Mr. Erdogan clearly and correctly stated, unless Hamas accepts Israel's reality, Hamas as

---

1 Sebnem Arsu and Ethan Bronner, "Gaza Premier in Turkey, in First Official Trip Abroad," *The New York Times*, January 2, 2012, http://www.nytimes.com/2012/01/03/world/middleeast/hamas-ismail-haniya-gaza-visits-turkey.html.

an organization will eventually be marginalized even by its own followers, the majority of whom want to put an end to the debilitating conflict with Israel that has led to nowhere but more pain and suffering.[2] Repeated polls conducted over the past year have clearly revealed growing support for the PA while Hamas' popularity shrinks. Hamas recognizes that it needs to change its strategy towards Israel and that Turkey can play an increasingly important role by helping Hamas' leadership take the final leap toward peace negotiations with Israel. Such an effort on Turkey's part is most timely because intense internal deliberations among Hamas' leaders about the pros and cons of ending militant resistance against Israel are taking place, which also remains a point of contention within the unity negotiations between Hamas and the Palestinian Authority.

More than any other party, Turkey has earned the trust and confidence of Hamas by being the first to invite to Ankara Hamas' political guru, Khaled Meshal, more than four years ago.[3] Even though Hamas has been designated as a terrorist organization by the US and the EU, Turkey has remained a vocal and ardent supporter of the organization ever since. In fact, Ankara has done so even at the expense of undermining its relations with Israel, especially since the Mavi Marmara incident on May 31st, 2010 in which nine activists (eight Turks and one Turkish-American citizen) were killed by Israeli soldiers. It is at this particular juncture that Turkey is perfectly positioned to bring Hamas in line with the Palestinian Authority due to the fact that: a) Hamas' political base in Damascus is in tatters due to the upheaval in Syria and is seeking a new political base outside Gaza; b) Iran, Hamas' main benefactor, is under tremendous international economic and political pressure because of its suspected pursuit of a nuclear weapons program; and c) Egypt's Muslim Brotherhood, Hamas' political supporter, is marred in a continuing struggle with the military over power-sharing, but gave up violence long ago to get to this point—an abject lesson for Hamas.

Notwithstanding the victories of Islamic political parties in the elections held in Tunisia, Morocco, and Egypt (and however encouraging that might be to Hamas), none of these parties have gained national popularity because of their pronounced hatred and animosity toward Israel. They have won because they have focused on domestic issues—their ailing economy, health care, education, and human rights—and precisely because they did not resort to scapegoating Israel or the United States for their respective country's ailments, a habitual practice of which the Arab youth is weary. Hamas knows its limitations and will not be carried away by the illusion of the "Islamic Spring." Israel will not be wished away and no party to the Israeli-Arab

---

2 "Poll: Most Palestinians want peace with Israel," *Haaretz*, June 20, 2010, http://www.haaretz.com/news/diplomacy-defense/poll-most-palestinians-want-peace-with-israel-1.297196.

3 Amberin Zaman, "Turkey Allows Hamas Visit," *Los Angeles Times*, February 17, 2006, http://articles.latimes.com/2006/feb/17/world/fg-hamas17.

conflict appreciates that better than Hamas, especially following the 2008/2009 Israeli incursions into Gaza. This further explains why Hamas is seriously deliberating abandoning violence against Israel as a means by which to realize Palestinian statehood.

Mr. Erdogan himself might well think that this is the age of Islamism and further enforce the general perception, in and outside of Turkey, that he favors any organization or country with strong Islamic credentials over others, regardless of the conflicting issues involved. However, Mr. Erdogan is realistic enough to understand that Turkey's continued economic developments and future leadership role in the Middle East depend on its ability to reconcile between the conflicting parties in the region. In particular, improved relations with Israel are one of the prerequisites for achieving that objective. Should Ankara continue to support Hamas without attempting to moderate its attitude toward Israel, Ankara will not only forsake the opportunity to lead but will be labeled as an obstructionist, especially in the eyes of the Arab-Sunni states that Turkey is trying to court, at a time when the entire region is in the process of geopolitical realignment.

Ankara can be sure that Iran will strongly and continuously encourage Hamas to hold onto its anti-Israel line under the pretext of serving the Palestinians' cause. In fact, Iran is only looking to serve its regional ambitions and will go to great lengths to protect its national interests, especially by supporting its surrogates such as Hamas and Hezbollah in carrying out its bidding. It is time for Turkey to realize that Tehran's and Ankara's national interests do not coincide and that in fact, the two countries may soon be on a collision course not only over post-Bashar Assad's Syria but over their overall regional ambitions. If Ankara considers regional stability central to its own national interests, then Turkey must spare no efforts to wean Hamas off of Tehran. Should Turkey decide to act in this direction, it can certainly count on both the US' and the EU's support.

Turkey is well-positioned to persuade Hamas to renounce violence, which is a prerequisite to becoming an active partner in the peace negotiations, and at the same time, to provide Hamas' leadership with the political cover they need to transition from a militant to a non-violent resistance movement. Once the label of terrorist organization is removed, Turkey may then invite Khaled Meshal to move his political headquarters from Damascus to Ankara. In so doing, Ankara will not only further distance Hamas from Iran but will help legitimize Hamas in the eyes of the US and the EU. Moreover, Ankara will be in a strong position to assert itself as a significant player in the Israeli-Palestinian peace process while beginning to mend its relations with Israel.

Regional leadership is not a given and it cannot be built on divisions and discords. Turkey must earn the regional leadership role it seeks to play. There is no better time than now for Ankara to use its influence on Hamas to make a crucial contribution to the Israeli-Palestinian peace process while enhancing its leadership role in a region in transformation.

THE ARAB UPRISING: AN IMPEDIMENT OR AN OPPORTUNITY FOR PEACE?

AUGUST 13, 2012

There is an ongoing debate in and outside of Israel as to whether or not this is the right time to forge peace with the Palestinians in light of the regional upheavals and instability. The peace process, at this juncture, is hopelessly frozen while the expansion of Israeli settlements and the continued internal Palestinian strife and factionalism increasingly dim the prospect of reaching an agreement. That said, the Arab Spring, which has triggered the rise of the Arab youth against their governments and has been accompanied by uncertainty, is not an impediment but an opportunity to solve the Israeli-Palestinian conflict based on a two-state solution. The reality on the ground strongly suggests that maintaining the status quo will be particularly detrimental to Israel.

Those inside the Netanyahu government who suggest that now is not the right time to seek a peace agreement with the Palestinians because of the regional turmoil and the existential threats that Israel now faces are both misguided and disingenuous. On the contrary, given the threats from Iran and its surrogate Hezbollah and the potential consequences of a failed state in Syria, it is a particularly critical moment for Israel to forge peace with the Palestinians. By doing so, Israel would be in a position to focus on the vastly more serious threats emanating from its real adversaries[4] and would prevent the rise of a Palestinian fifth column, should Israel become mired in these regional conflicts. To enhance their positions, those who oppose peace now offer three faulty arguments to justify their stance.

First, the Palestinians cannot be trusted and Israel "correctly" points to the precedents of the partial disengagement from the West Bank between 1993 and 2000, the complete withdrawal from southern Lebanon in 2000, and the withdrawal from Gaza in 2005. From the Israeli perspective, all of these moments attest to the Palestinians' inability or unwillingness to forge a permanent peace, despite having ample opportunities.

Second, due to Palestinian factionalism and infighting, there is no credible partner with whom Israel can negotiate as the Palestinians have been unable to

---

4 David Ignatius, "Israel's Arab Spring problem," *The Washington Post*, July 5, 2012. http://www. washingtonpost.com/opinions/david-ignatius-israels-arab-spring-problem/2012/07/05/gJQAV5JrRW_story.html.

sustain a unity government. The Netanyahu government is convinced that even if an agreement is reached, it will still prove transient.

Third, there are extremist Palestinian groups, such as Hamas, Islamic Jihad and others, along with non-Palestinian factions, including Hezbollah and al-Qaeda, that are vehemently antagonistic toward Israel and remain committed to its destruction.

However, none of the three arguments above can pass careful scrutiny. These types of arguments are used as excuses and a cover for the Netanyahu government's deep conviction that the Jews have an inherent right to the whole "land of Israel." This remains an indefatigable nonstarter to reaching a peace agreement that requires significant territorial concessions, including the conversion of Jerusalem to the capital of both Israeli and Palestinian states. From the Netanyahu government's perspective, the conditions of no peace and no war that currently prevail are preferable to a compromise of the Jews' historical rights, and through a strong and determined will, Israel will eventually triumph.

In light of the reality on the ground, which both the Israelis and the Palestinians alike must face by virtue of their inevitable coexistence, Israel must act now because the passage of time may well be to its detriment, if not its very existence. There are three critical issues that increasingly work against Israel.

Considering Israel's demographic situation, its evolutionary path has shifted radically as emigration from Israel over the past two decades (about one million) is roughly equal to the immigration into Israel for the same period.[5] This, along with low birth rates relative to the Palestinian population, continues to erode the sustainability of Israel's national character as a Jewish state. Should this growing demographic imbalance between the Jewish and Palestinian populations continue,[6] Israel will be forced to either establish a single state (an unacceptable proposition for them as it will instantly make the Jewish population a minority) or resort to apartheid policies that will be vehemently rejected by the international community.

In recent years, Israel has been fortunate that Gaza and the West Bank were generally quiet with limited resistance to the occupation and launched only marginal rocket attacks from Gaza that the Israeli military was able to handle with ease. Maintaining the occupation, however, and the continuance of the creeping expansion of the settlements,

5 Joseph Chamie and Barry Mirkin, "The million missing Israelis – Israeli emigration," *Foundation for Middle East Peace*, July 5, 2011. http://www.fmep.org/analysis/analysis/the-million-missing-israelis-israeli-emigration.

6 Sergio Della Pergola, interviewed by Murray Fromson, *The Jewish Journal*, April 8, 2010. http://www.afhu.org/files/HUArticles/The Arabs are multiplying twice as fast as the Israelis.pdf.

coupled with the uprisings of Arab youth against *their own governments,* now make it only a matter of time before the Palestinians will be inspired, if not forced, to rise *against the occupation.*[7] They will not remain indefinitely passive, as they clearly see that the longer they wait, the more of their land will be consumed, resulting in an irreversible reality on the ground that will deny the rise of an independent and viable state.

Moreover, Israel will continue to face intensifying pressure from the international community due to the perpetuation of the status quo, which will dramatically increase Israel's isolation. For the United States and the European Union, who continue to be steadfast supporters of Israel, the lack of progress has a destabilizing effect on the region, which directly and indirectly impacts *their national strategic interests* and undermines Israel's national security. Israel should not be surprised if its closest allies, especially the US, decide to advance their own frameworks for peace largely based on prior Israeli-Palestinian negotiations in an attempt to save Israel from charting its own disastrous path.

In a broader context, Israel's current enemies, specifically Iran and Hezbollah, will continue to exploit the Israeli-Palestinian conflict to their advantage. To counteract this encroaching threat, Israel can at least begin to neutralize its antagonists' positions by taking steps that open the door for a negotiated solution and normalization of relations with the Arab states by accepting the Arab Peace Initiative as a basis for negotiations. While this strategy may not initially and necessarily change the principle objection to Israel's very existence by actors such as Iran and Hezbollah, Israel could shift the geopolitical conditions in the region in its favor. As I was convincingly told time and time again by top Arab officials, the Arab states are prepared to move toward establishing full diplomatic relations with Israel once an Israeli-Palestinian peace is achieved. They cite the changing dynamics in the region in the wake of the Arab Spring and the ensuing battle between Sunnis, led by Saudi Arabia and Turkey, and Shiites, led by Iran who seeks regional hegemony.

Despite the complex situation that Israel finds itself in, the basic question remains: how much longer can it sustain its present course without experiencing horrific and self-inflicted wounds? Israel must face the inevitable now while it is still in a strong position to negotiate an agreement with the Palestinians, a population that has, and can continue to, withstand the test of time. Unlike the precipitous withdrawal from Southern Lebanon and Gaza, any agreement with the Palestinians should be made with the Palestinian Authority in the West Bank and should be based on a *quid pro quo* that would involve

---

7 For another analysis of this situation, see Nathan Thrall, "The Third Intifada Is Inevitable," *The New York Times*, June 22, 2012, http://www.nytimes.com/2012/06/24/opinion/sunday/the-third-intifada-is-inevitable.html?_r=0.

phased withdrawals from the West Bank over a few years in order to foster mutual trust and normalization of relations *while ensuring Israel's national security.*

Set against the context of the Arab Spring, Israel remains an oasis of stability with its economic, military, and technological advantages continuing to strengthen over time.[8] The inability of the Palestinians to change the dynamics in their favor has deepened the Israelis' complacency while removing any sense of urgency to solve the conflict, as they remain intoxicated by their military prowess and the deceptive calm before the storm. Simply put, passively waiting for the region to achieve a modicum of stability while Israel further entrenches itself in the territories is a non-starter as the Arab upheavals are not a fading phenomenon and will remain an engine of change for years, if not decades, to come. The Palestinian's turn will come sooner than expected.

I must emphasize that the Palestinians, by their own violent actions and hostile public utterances, have directly contributed to the Israelis' skepticism and deepening of their conviction that the Palestinians are neither partners to be trusted nor are they a population with whom they can negotiate a lasting peace. That said, it is up to Israel not to allow past experiences to blur its vision for the future, and it must now chart its own future course by ending the occupation under specific "rules of disengagement" with the Palestinian Authority. Israel must *never* abandon the principles of equality and human rights regardless of race, color, or religion, as they are the very basis on which the state arose from the ashes of the Holocaust.

Netanyahu will eventually have to answer to the Israeli public as to what he has achieved over the past four years. The Israelis must now determine whether or not Netanyahu has made the conflict with the Palestinians considerably worse since he took office in 2009 and what price Israel will have to pay for his misguided and ominous policies.

8 Fareed Zakaria, "Under Netanyahu, Israel is stronger than ever," *The Washington Post*, May 9, 2012. http://www.washingtonpost.com/opinions/under-netanyahu-israel-is-stronger-than-ever/2012/05/09/gIQAcTH2DU_story.html.

RELIGION

RELIGION

ARAB SPRING AND REVIVAL OF ISLAMIC STATE

Few Muslims would dispute the notion that Islam should guide their private as well as public lives, since the Quran and the *Sunna* (the tradition of Prophet Muhammad) –the two primary sources of Islam's religious law, or *Shari'a* – provide instructions on virtually every aspect of life. Muslims differ, however, on the varying readings of what *Shari'a* means, which has led to the diverse schools of Islamic jurisprudence, or *Fiqh*. The wide spectrum of *Fiqh* schools in Sunni or Shiite Islam vary across two key dimensions: interpretation (verbatim vs. socially-conditioned interpretation) and authority (identity of those qualified to make interpretation and the nature of their political power).

The Arab Spring exposed both the hypocrisy of the established religious authorities, who issued *fatwas* against the pro-democracy protests in Egypt, Libya, Syria, and Yemen, and the bankruptcy of the radical militants' ideology. Arabs who protested in the streets across religious, age, and gender lines were motivated by aspirations for the universal values of freedom and human rights– a consensus even the staunchest of Islamists cannot ignore.

In the matrix, Sunni schools endorse whoever the Muslim community chooses to lead it as the legitimate ruler, while Shiite Islam assigns religious and political leadership to the descendants of the Prophet (as infallible Imams), on behalf of which the Shiite scholars act as agents. Moderate Sunni schools (*Hanafi* and *Maliki*), as well as some Shiite schools adopt socially-conditioned interpretations based on logical deduction by scholars; while the conservative Sunni schools (*Hanbali*) adopt a strict, verbatim interpretation. In reality, however, the Islamic world has been divided into three classes: secular government that consigns religion to personal life (Egypt); ostensibly religious, but essentially secular government that sanctions the intrusive authority of clerics (Saudi Arabia); and outright religious government (Iran).

Ironically, rivaling Sunni Saudi Arabia and Shiite Iran invoke *Shari'a* to maintain their dictatorial regimes and oppress political freedoms using the same maxim – rebelling against authority is rebelling against what God has instituted, as sovereignty belongs to God and not to the people. Combined with discriminatory practices against women and non-Muslim minorities, as well as the electoral victories of anti-Western Islamists based on the example of "one man, one vote, one time," in Sudan, Gaza, and Algeria, the notion that Islam and liberal democracy are incompatible gained popularity.

Shari'a has also been invoked for purposes other than domestic oppression. Iran's deception of the international community with regards to its nuclear program is believed to stem from the Shiite concept of *taqqiya* – permission for believers to hide the truth from nonbelievers to protect the religion – which is arguably justified in the Quran (3:28; 16:106). It is no wonder, then, that there are those who believe that Islam permits devout Muslims to deliberately lie to and cheat non-Muslims to promote the religion of Islam anytime and anywhere.

Even worse, *Shari'a* has been invoked by radical, militant Islamist groups, such as al-Qaeda, to justify committing terror attacks against non-Muslim civilians in the West, as well as their fellow Muslims under the guise of Jihad. Here, Jihad is understood as the duty of every Muslim to wage war against all non-Muslims with the ultimate aim of the ruling the world.

These patterns of abusing *Shari'a* by authoritarian Muslim rulers and militant groups bring us back to the two key dimensions of *Fiqh* schools: interpretation and authority. Works of radical Islamic theorists as well as regime-co-opted religions are essentially the product of a selective interpretation process that at one time adopts explanations provided by medieval clerics, and at another makes an independent interpretation, according to the current political agenda and self-interests, not reason.

Less known, however, is a great legacy of sensible Islamic scholars who warned against this abusive process a long time ago. Muhammad Abdu, the enlightened Islamic scholar of the nineteenth century, viewed reason as the ultimate virtue of Islam; therefore, any dogma contradicting morals or the core values of Islam – justice, consultative governance, and mercy – should be ruled out. One authority, Ali Abdel-Raziq of the early twentieth century, argued persuasively in his 1925 seminal treatise, *Islam and the Foundations of Governance*, that Islam does not suggest any particular type of government, religious or otherwise, because the Prophet's divine mission has been to establish a community of believers, not a body politic.[1]

1 Werner Ende and Udo Steinbach, *Islam in the World Today: A Handbook of Politics, Religion, Culture, and Society* (Ithaca, NY: Cornell University Press, 2010), 101.

The relevance of the above discussion to the ongoing, groundbreaking developments in the Arab-Islamic world and the West cannot be exaggerated. On the one hand, the Islamists have an unprecedented window of opportunity that, if taken properly, would allow them not only to revive the religion of Islam in a constructive and beneficial way, but also to present the world with an example to be emulated. Islamist forces in the Arab world should introduce a face of Islam that shows the deeper and truer meaning of Jihad – one's internal struggle to maintain faith, and the struggle to improve the Muslim community. This is especially true at a time when the people are becoming wary about allowing the boundaries of politics and religion to blur, raising legitimate questions about what Islamist rule has brought to Iran (oppressed people whose nation's resources are squandered by the political elite and wasted on exporting terrorism, building nuclear armaments, and revolution-export business) or the Sudan (poor, oppressed people having their nation split into two after a long, bloody, and losing war).

Initial signs in the right direction have already appeared in revolutionary Egypt where ideologues of *Jamat al-Islamiyya*, who took up arms against the Mubarak regime in the 1980s and the 1990s, now search for a form of Islamic liberalism that is inclusive of other political forces in society.[2] In Tunisia and Libya, where Islamists are expected to dominate the next elections, leaders and citizens tend to reject the Saudi and Taliban models, seen as sheer dictatorships, and opt instead for the Malaysian and Indonesian ones that combine Islam and modernity.[3] If this approach is sincere and given enough effort to mature into coherent policy, it would lead to the emergence of a democratic Islamic state model that would respond to the reforms Muslim societies require, and turn Samuel Huntington's clash of civilizations prophecy into a mere academic discourse.

On the other hand, the economic turbulence that many Western democracies are experiencing and the growing gap between the rich and poor in most economically advanced nations raises questions about the sustainability of the world's economic system. Islamic banking is becoming an increasingly more attractive alternative since its interest-free finance – based on *Shari'a* prohibition of payment for loans of money – responds to the very dilemmas that caused the current global economic crisis: lending capital and mortgage transactions. This could lead the already growing Islamic banking system to thrive worldwide, and offer some example of modifying business practices with the rules of *Shari'a*.

2 Emad Mekay, "In Egypt, Islamists Reach Out to Wary Secularists," *The New York Times*, September 21, 2011. http://www.nytimes.com/2011/09/22/world/middleeast/in-egypt-islamists-reach-out-to-wary-secularists.html.
3 Anthony Shadid and David D. Kirkpatrick, "Activists in Arab World Vie to Define Islamic State," *The New York Times*, September 29, 2011. http://www.nytimes.com/2011/09/30/world/middleeast/arab-debate-pits-islamists-against-themselves.html.

Despite the decades-long abuse of *Shari'a* to justify oppression, deception, and terror, and despite the fact that democracy is a Western-born concept, Islam and liberal democracy are essentially congruent. In his 2004 book *Islam and the Challenge of Democracy*, Khaled Abou El Fadl of UCLA brilliantly departs from the traditional approach to this case – i.e., asserting that ideas of representation between leaders and the led are commended in the Quran (42:38) – and adheres to the core values of Islam, including diversity and justice, which resonate with those of liberal democracy and human rights. It is these works of Abdu, Abdel-Raziq, and Abu El Fadl, and their application to contemporary concrete needs of the people that would lead to the revival of an Islamic world that lives in peace and could potentially make a significant contribution to civilization.

The rising Arab youth want to be free and live with dignity without abandoning their Islamic roots. Thus, it is not the mere adoption of Western values of freedom and human rights that will determine the successes of the newly emerging Arab regimes as a result of the Arab Spring, but how well these values are incorporated into the Islamic way of life without violence and unending strife.

TRANSCENDING FALSE PERCEPTIONS

In a recent article,[4] I argued that Israel and the Muslim Brotherhood (MB) in Egypt should accept the fact each other exist and will continue to exist in the same neighborhood indefinitely, both as an acknowledgement of their mutual realities and as a way to end the Israeli-Palestinian conflict and improve Israeli-Egyptian relations. Nonetheless, deeper than an acceptance of reality and beyond the MB is the need for a rapprochement between Israel and the Islamic Arab world, which must be based not on necessity but on the desirability of coexistence between Muslims and Jews.

The Quran provides the very source that Islamist extremists draw deliberate textual misinterpretations from to justify the notion of an eternal and inevitable struggle between Muslims and Jews. That said, religious reconciliation between the two sides cannot occur unless the Israeli-Palestinian conflict is settled on the basis of a two-state solution—a solution which necessarily requires the cessation of the occupation, which has provided the rationale and justification for Jihad against Israel.

Israel and the Islamic Arab world must coexist, as coexistence simply is not optional and the alternative will only prolong the strife and bloodshed between the two sides. A telling example is the situation in Jerusalem and Hebron, where Muslims and Jews are *religiously stuck* in the same place, live side by side, and cannot entertain the idea of excluding the other or harming each other's holy shrines without incurring unacceptable consequences. Some Muslims argue that such coexistence is derived by necessity and not by choice. But note that an important feature of *al-Isra wa al-Miraj* – the Prophet Mohamed's prayer with all previous prophets, including Abraham and Moses, at the al-Aqsa Mosque in Jerusalem – implies the inclusive nature of the divine message.

If hardcore Islamists and extreme, right-wing Israeli activists maintain that Islam orthodoxy is inherently anti-Jewish and need further convincing that this is not the case, they must transcend their false perceptions and look deeper into the Quran to find that coexistence between Jews and Muslims is natural to the teachings of Islam. There are Quranic texts in favor of coexistence; literal interpretations taken out of their specific contexts, however, can undermine relations, as they have in the past, between Muslims and Jews. Importantly, the broader picture that the Quran provides explicitly recognizes the Jews as a nation worthy of respect.

---

4 See "Israel and the Muslim Brotherhood: Facing the Bitter-Sweet Reality," page 51.

For Muslims, the message of the Prophet Muhammad is an extension and continuation of the message brought from God by Moses and other Biblical prophets (Quran 2:285), the belief in whom is an article of faith (Quran 2:136). Not only Jews but Christians as well are referred to repeatedly as People of the Book, and the Quran constantly reminds Muslims that "among" the People of the Book are those who believe and do righteous deeds (Quran 3:113–115). The word "among" is an important modifier which is conveniently overlooked by many readers of the Quran today. The *Sunna* – the tradition of the Prophet Muhammad, together with the Quran's two primary sources of Islamic *Shari'a* – even declares that Muslims and Jews form one *Umma* (nation) in the 622 Charter of Medina between the Muslims and the residents of Medina.[5]

The Quran, however, is not a list from which to pick-and-choose. Rather, it presents a coherent teaching that preaches peace as much as it calls upon its adherents to resist all forms of injustice, including the use of force if deemed necessary – much like the Old and New Testaments. Despite Quranic permission for Muslims to fight in self-defense, Muslims were warned not to go beyond defending themselves to the extent of transgression. The following Quranic verse permits Muslims to defend against those who attack them: "If then anyone transgresses the prohibition against you, transgress likewise against him." (Quran 2: 194). For this reason, under Islamic teachings the Palestinians and other Muslims can justify their violent resistance to the Israeli occupation. Hence, from this perspective, only an end to the Israeli occupation will make peace both possible and desirable. According to Islamic teachings, if the Muslims learn that their enemy desires peace and is willing to cease all forms of aggression, Islam commands them to agree to their enemy's request: "But if they [the enemies] incline towards peace, you (also) incline towards peace and trust in God." (Quran 8:61).

Islamist extremists might find it comforting to invoke Quranic verses to justify acts of terrorism against the Jews. But committing acts of terrorism in the name of Islam – most recently the random killing in France of two Jewish boys, their father and another Jewish child[6] – is actually an insult to Islamic teachings, which considers all life forms as sacred and condemns terrorizing and killing innocent people, even in times of war. Nor for that matter do the continued Israeli occupation and the subjugation of the Palestinians to daily indignities enhance the image of Jewish

---

5 R.B. Sergeant, "The 'Constitution of Medina,'" *Islamic Quarterly* 8, no. 1 (1964): 3-17.

6 Scott Sayare and Steven Erlanger, "Gunman May Have Filmed Attack at French School," *The New York Times*, March 20, 2012, http://www.nytimes.com/2012/03/21/world/europe/jewish-school-shooting-in-france.html?pagewanted=all.

teachings. Religious belief, be it Jewish, Christian, or Muslim, was not meant to provide a cover for any injustices. On the contrary, the three major religions strongly advocate brotherhood, justice, and peace.

There are many skeptical Israelis who understandably do not believe that an Islamic world which cannot live in peace within itself (noting the perpetual conflict between Sunnis and Shiites) will accept Israel as a Jewish state. They point out the butchering of Muslims by Muslims in Sudan, Iraq, Libya, and now Syria, which strongly suggests, from their perspective, that violence is inherent to Islamic religion and culture. I do not subscribe to this proposition for four reasons: a) the Quran's teachings consistently point to the contrary; b) neither violence nor extremism is exclusively Muslim (note European history from the time of the Inquisition to date); c) time and circumstances have changed as the Arab youth have now been awakened while focusing on their plight under despotic regimes, and no longer buy into the argument that Israel is the culprit behind their socio-economic and political plight; and d) the Muslim world has come to terms with the unequivocal reality of Israel, with the exception of a tiny fraction of Islamist militants opposing Israel compared to the Muslim world's population of 1.4 billion.

Conversely, for Israel to peacefully exist in the midst of the Arab world it too must come to terms with the changing political wind and the Palestinian reality by removing the stigma of occupation. Israel is powerful enough to take the calculated risk of putting to the test the Arab states' protestation that they will seek peace if only a mutually acceptable and just solution is found to the Israeli-Palestinian conflict. Indeed, to suggest that the relationship between Islamic-leaning Arab states and Israel is irreconcilable flies in the face of reality. Israel should remember that it was Saudi Arabia, one of the most conservative among the Islamic countries, that advanced the Arab Peace Initiative in 2002 and it is Israel that still, a decade later, refuses to embrace it.

Finally, there are two unmitigated facts, the realization of which, in my view, is inevitable. The first is that the rise of Islamic forces in the Arab states has already taken place in Tunisia and Egypt, will most likely come to Libya and Syria, and will assuredly further expand to other Arab states. The second fact is that Israel will maintain its ability to defend itself and would unleash any weapons at its disposal against those who pose an existential threat, such as Iran and militant Islamist organizations (who would do so at their own peril).

To disabuse both the Jewish and Arab/Muslim publics of their false perception about each other, Jewish and Muslim religious scholars should engage in an open dialogue. They can now use modern communication tools for all to see and hear how and why the two sides must accept the inevitable and reconcile their differences, including the future of Jerusalem, while using religious teachings to make their case.

Indeed, what is needed here is a change in the public narrative before we can change public perceptions of each other. This will, over time, provide policy makers, be they religious or secular, the political cover they need to pursue reconciliation. The question now is how much more anguish and uncertainty must Israel and the Islamic Arab world further endure to accept this inevitability?

PREVENTING SUNNI-SHIITE SCHISM FROM HIJACKING THE ARAB SPRING

MAY 29, 2012

In April of this year, I wrote[7] that the upheaval in Syria has turned into a battleground between the Sunni axis, led by Turkey and Saudi Arabia, and the Shiite axis, led by Iran. As events continue to unfold in the region – particularly the Sunni Islamists' monopolization of the political processes in Egypt, Libya, and Tunisia plus the belligerent Saudi-Iranian exchange in Syria and Bahrain – what is increasingly visible is that the liberal, democracy-seeking Arab Spring is being hijacked by radical Islamists on both sides, risking major conflagration between the two sects of Islam.

The dispute between Sunnis (who make up the vast majority of the world's Muslims) and Shiites is not faith-related, but is rather essentially political about how the Caliph should be appointed and the nature of political power that religious scholars should have.[8] Much like Europe in the 1500s and 1600s, with theology intertwined with geopolitics, the conflict was sustained for a millennium from the seventh to the seventeenth century and witnessed the conflict between the Shiite Safavid dynasty in Persia and the Sunni Ottoman dynasty in Turkey.[9] It was not until the Islamic Revolution in Iran in 1979 and the Iraq-Iran War (1980–1988), culminating with the Iraq War in 2003, that the relationship between the Arab world and Iran was again re-framed in the context of the Sunni-Shiite schism. The emergence of a Shiite government in post-Saddam Iraq, discriminating against its Sunni citizens, and the ensuing Sunni insurgency terrorizing the Shiite majority only added fuel to the fire. The high hopes accompanying the advent of the Arab Spring, that the youth uprising would make a smooth transition to a liberal democracy, are gradually fading away.

After the Muslim Brotherhood (MB) in Egypt won a decisive victory in the country's first free elections, it fielded a presidential candidate and the legislature it dominated drafted a law that is restructuring the Supreme Constitutional Court in a way that gives parliament greater control over its affairs.[10] Being the best-financed and

---

7 See "Syria: The Battleground Between Sunnis and Shiites," page 103.

8 Ramazan Gözen, "Sunni-Shiite conflict: fact or fuss?," *Today's Zaman*, February 12, 2012. http://www.todayszaman.com/newsDetail_getNewsById.action?newsId=271224.

9 For further information, please see PM Holt, Ann KS Lambton, and Bernard Lewis, *The Central Islamic lands from pre-Islamic times to the first World War* (New York: Cambridge University Press, 1977)..

10 "Egypt constitution court blasts draft legislation curtailing its power," *Ahram Online*, May 16, 2012. http://english.ahram.org.eg/NewsContent/1/64/41795/Egypt/Politics-/Egypt-constitution-court-blasts-draft-legislation-.aspx.

organized group, the MB is likely to successfully monopolize the political process. A rational MB, one might argue, could make some concessions and employ a cautious approach, but even this restrains the MB in introducing real political freedoms because of two major factors: 1) the reluctance of the old guard of the MB to democratize, lest they lose a historical opportunity to transform Egypt into the model Islamic state; and 2) the competition with the ultra-conservative Salafists – unexpectedly ranked second in the parliament – whose challenge of the MB's religious credentials forced it to talk about how and when they will implement *Sharia* law.[11]

On the other hand, the Arab Spring gave Shiite Arab minorities the opportunity to rise and demand political freedoms and civil rights, which they have been generally denied in the Sunni-dominated Arab Gulf monarchies. For its part, Iran misses no opportunity to foment the Shiite unrest where it failed for three decades to export its Islamic revolution. Ironically, Iran is doing this at a time when it gives full, unconditional support to the oppression practiced by the Shiite crescent member regimes of Syria, Lebanon, and Iraq at the expense of the rights – and lives – of the Sunnis in these countries. Wary of the implications, the bastion of Sunni Islam, Saudi Arabia, is building alliances with states that share its outlook in a Sunni axis to combat the Shiite arc, including the Gulf States (to the extent that it considers a union with Bahrain)[12] and is extending full cooperation to Egypt, Jordan, and Turkey.

The dilemma, however, is that this same Saudi Arabia is seen, by virtue of its position as the guardian of Sunni Islam, as one whose response to the Arab Spring was limited to introducing only modest reforms. For that purpose, it is reported that Saudi Arabia has been engaged in efforts to dissuade the Bahraini monarch from introducing substantive political reforms. Also, and more importantly, it might provide the MB in Egypt with the economic assistance that the country desperately needs in return for a full commitment to the Sunni axis.[13] This might discourage the MB, as many Egyptian scholars attest, from introducing real democratic reforms, especially at a time when Saudi Arabia is suspected of being the primary source of funding for the Salafists[14] who adopt a Wahabi-like ideology and whose detestation of Shiites is only second to its

---

11 Sarah A. Topol, "Egypt's Salafi Surge," *Foreign Policy*, January 4, 2012. http://www.foreignpolicy.com/articles/2012/01/04/egypt_s_salafi_surge.

12 Andrew Hammond and Angus McDowall, "Saudi and Bahrain expected to seek union: minister," *Reuters*, May 13, 2012, http://www.reuters.com/article/2012/05/14/us-gulf-union-idUSBRE84C07120120514.

13 Nayla Razzouk, "Egypt to Receive $4 Billion Economic Aid From Saudi Arabia, SPA Reports," *Bloomberg*, May 21, 2012, http://www.bloomberg.com/news/2011-05-21/saudi-arabia-gives-4-billion-egyptian-economic-aid-spa-says.html.

14 "Anti-Christian violence sparks fears of rising Salafi influence," *France 24*, December 5, 2011. http://www.france24.com/en/20110512-egypt-christian-muslim-violence-sparks-fears-rising-salafi-influence.

distaste toward infidels.[15] Unfortunately, the net result is that the Arab Spring, which gave rise to the strong camp of Sunni Islamists, is being hijacked by the Sunni-Shiite schism whose focus is to perpetuate their own brand of religious authority over the affairs of the state, regardless of the peoples' wishes.

To avoid a catastrophic scenario in which the two sects of Islam clash in a long, debilitating, and bloody conflict to realize their political ambitions – read authoritarian aspirations of their rulers – the mission of the Sunni Arab world is twofold. First, the governments of Saudi Arabia and Egypt in particular should make every effort to present a type of Islamic governance that does not alienate other political forces in their respective society. An inclusive system, combined with sustainable development projects to alleviate poverty consistent with Islamic teachings, would not only avoid a sooner-or-later counter-revolutionary explosion, but would also provide an example to the Iranian people to counter the Mullahs in Tehran.

Second, the youths' part in the Sunni Arab world is to reclaim the fundamental underpinnings of their revolution. In Egypt, which may well provide the microcosm of what could take place in the rest of the Arab world, many Egyptians have already started to express regrets for voting for the MB and other Islamist parties in the last parliamentary elections,[16] and for good reason. Islamists did not deliver what they promised: a decent living for the average Egyptian while corruption and crimes are curbed. The youth should learn from their mistakes in the latest elections by closing ranks, running united electorally, and embarking on a massive campaign to protect the democratic, civil nature of the new Egypt by engaging the vast majority of the Egyptian people. Only constant pressure from the public will compel the MB and its candidate for President, Mohamed Morsi, should he win the runoff election next month, to respond to the public's demands for real reforms and navigate a middle path combining Islam with democracy.

No less important is the role of the Shiite Arab youth. In Bahrain, Saudi Arabia, and elsewhere in the Gulf States, the youth should not allow themselves to be exploited by the devious Iranian leadership. Instead, *they should demand their political and civil rights from within the system* and not allow outside instigators to undermine the national security and integrity of their home countries.

Consistent with Israel's national interests is to prevent a hegemonic Iran from emerging. Prime Minister Netanyahu should use the unprecedented mandate he

15 Ed Husain, "Why Egypt's Salafis Are Not the Amish," *Council on Foreign Relations*, December 1, 2011. http://blogs.cfr.org/husain/2011/12/01/why-egypt%E2%80%99s-salafis-are-not-the-amish/.

16 David D. Kirkpatrick and Mayy El Sheikh, "In Streets and Online, Campaign Fever in Egypt," *The New York Times*, May 20, 2012, http://www.nytimes.com/2012/05/21/world/middleeast/in-streets-and-online-campaign-fever-in-egypt.html.

currently has in the Knesset to take a serious stand on peace with the Palestinians, especially now as the Sunni-Shiite conflict is intensifying, instead of his futile "wait-and-see" approach. Peace based on a two-state solution would not only empower the Sunni axis (and allow extending cooperation with the Gulf and North Africa's Arab states) but would also maintain Israel's national identity as a Jewish and democratic state which is seriously threatened by further prolonging the Israeli-Palestinian conflict.

It is within this dual platform that the Arab Sunni world can maintain its coherence and present an alternative to their societies by sharing Islam's values of freedom, justice, and human rights, which have thus far been squashed by blind Islamic Sunni and Shiite orthodoxy, whose time is surely running out.

ENCOMPASSING THE ARAB SPRING

ENCOMPASSING THE ARAB SPRING

THE ARAB UPRISING

CONDITIONS THAT WILL DOMINATE FUTURE DISCOURSE

MARCH 11, 2011

Promoting democratic reforms in Egypt and throughout the Arab world is critical under any circumstances and no effort should be spared by the people—in partnership with their governments whenever possible—to bring about political reforms consistent with their aspirations. Foreign governments and human rights organizations can and should provide assistance only as requested, bearing in mind three critical requirements to lasting reforms. Since the governance and traditions of each Arab state differ, there is no single template of political reforms applicable to all. Rapid reforms without transitional periods to allow for the development of civil society and secular political parties could lead to further destabilization. And finally, political reforms are not sustainable—and might even backfire—unless they are concurrently accompanied by substantial economic development programs that can provide immediate benefits.

NO SINGLE TEMPLATE FOR REFORMS, BUT MANY COMMON DENOMINATORS

The breathtaking developments in the Arab world seem to have taken many parties by surprise, and speculations about how the Middle East will look in the future run the gamut. There are those who argue that revolutions against dictatorships, even when they succeed, do not guarantee lasting democratic political reforms. Many former Soviet Republics (especially those with Islamic roots) offer glaring examples, such as Turkmenistan under President Gurbanguly Berdymukhamedov, Uzbekistan under President Islam Karimov, or Tajikistan under President Emomali Rahmon. These and others have become one-man rule, stifling political freedom while often applying ruthless methods to maintain their grip on power. Others contend that regardless of how the events unfold, the Arab world will continue to undergo transformational changes of historic proportions, and that Arab governments have no choice but to heed their public's yearning for greater freedoms. And then there are those who assert that any reforms the Arab regimes are ultimately willing to undertake will be superficial, varying in degree and duration, and designed to pacify the revolutionaries. They insist that entrenched constituencies such as the military and Islamic organizations in the region remain determined to shape events according to their political agendas, and that the only certainty about the future is, in fact, uncertainty.

These arguments and others bear a degree of cogency that cannot readily be dismissed. That said, there are certain conditions created by the uprisings that will remain constant and will impact each Arab country differently. Moreover, regardless of how firm their grip on power may be today, no Arab government will be immune to some degree of meaningful change. But the sooner they understand the potency and long-lasting implications of these new conditions, the less blood will be shed and the smoother and more peaceful the transitional period will be.

Those who never expected Arab youth to rise against their authoritarian governments were proven wrong. The Arab youth of today is not the same youth of a generation ago. This new generation has been exposed to the world at large; they have risen against oppression, deprivation and stagnation, and they no longer want to live in submission to corrupt leaders and governments. To assume that Arab youth will indefinitely remain subjugated to them *is nothing short of an insult* to a people who have contributed so much to civilization and enlightenment. No Arab government, however oppressive, will ever be in a position to completely shut down their youths' access to the outside world and stifle their yearning for freedom. Regardless of how youth uprisings fluctuate in intensity, they are not a passing phenomenon. They will last for years and wind down only when Arab regimes commit to and deliver on promises for constructive and permanent political and economic reforms, regardless of how long that might take.

The current Arab regimes must also remember that the youth uprisings are an indigenous movement; they were neither instigated by outside powers or groups, as some Arab leaders alluded, nor did the revolutionaries need to blame outside entities for their plight. The youth have pointed their fingers at the failure of their own governments. The revolting youth refuse to be distracted by the old empty slogans and contrived excuses that suggest chaos will dominate in the absence of the current leaders should they be ousted from power. Gone are the days when Arab leaders could ride the storm of public discontent by blaming Israel or the United States or former colonial powers for their trying existence. The people want their leaders to focus instead on addressing their grievances in earnest and not look for scapegoats, which only brought more deprivation and despair to their people.

In addition, the Arab uprising still represents only the beginning of a continuing wave of instability that is sweeping the region and will not subside by temporary economic measures. The latest example is Saudi Arabian King Abdullah's $37 billion welfare package for Saudi citizens and a 15 percent raise for government employees.[1] Another is the Bahraini government's payment in the sum of $2,650 to each family to buy their compliance and silence.[2] These are examples of an unsustainable approach governments take in their effort to quell public demands for greater freedom and social equality. The Arab regimes must realize that the public *does not want handouts, they want a voice.* They want to be heard, because they have the inherent right to be heard. They want to live in dignity and will undoubtedly refuse to settle for their government's recent reactionary display of pursuing social justice.

There is no cure-all that will fit the needs for change in different Arab states. Monarchs and Emirs, the rulers of the Gulf States, Jordan, and Morocco will undoubtedly face serious challenges, but in the end—however many years that might take—they will be forced to accept, or will evolve toward (through expanded and successful democratic sustainable development programs) a constitutional monarchy, or a more highly democratic one. Other countries like Algeria, Tunisia, and Egypt may have to choose a republican form of government with powerful elected legislators led by a prime minister, with a strong military behind the scenes to guard against abuses of power. Still others like Libya, Yemen, and Sudan may end up dominated by a military clique for a number of years in an effort to reconcile different tribal demands while promoting some political and economic reforms. Syria may succeed to head off youth uprisings by initiating some political and economic reforms. Lebanon will remain a sectarian tinderbox, while the Palestinians will be emboldened to rise up in an effort to end the Israeli occupation, use international forums to bring pressure to bear on Israel, and build a more self-reliant economy (an important premise in the Fayyad Plan). Generally speaking, the transition in the Arab monarchies will be more peaceful than in other Arab states, but most will experience various degrees of violence. Regardless of the kind of government many Arab states will end up with, adherence to basic human rights and

1 Caryle Murphy, "Saudi Arabia's King Abudllah promises $36 billion in benefits," *Christian Science Monitor,* February 23, 2011, http://www.csmonitor.com/World/Middle-East/2011/0223/Saudi-Arabia-s-King-Abdullah-promises-36-billion-in-benefits.
2 "Bahrain doles out money to families," *Al Jazeera,* February 12, 2011, http://www.aljazeera.com/news/middleeast/2011/02/201121251854857192.html.

the removal of all emergency laws will be central to a more peaceful transition. No Arab government will be exempt from these requirements.

The Arab world will continue to undergo transformational changes of historic proportions led by determined youth committed to liberating themselves from the shackles of poverty. Every Arab regime must either heed their public's yearning for greater freedoms and economic developments, or likely be fundamentally challenged. Egypt offers a microcosm of the changes that have occurred and the kind of reforms that must be pursued. How the revolution in Egypt further evolves will have a direct and indirect impact on the rest of the Arab states, as Egypt has traditionally been—and will continue to be—the leader of the Arab world.

REALPOLITIK VERSUS POLITICAL IDEALS

MAY 2, 2011

First, I want to congratulate President Obama for bringing the only deserving end to Osama Bin Laden. This will send a clear message to every terrorist that America will remain relentless until we bring an end to the scourge of terrorism.

Notwithstanding the heroism of this act by our courageous armed forces, the Obama administration has appeared befuddled, slow-to-react, and inconsistent in its response to the awakening of the masses protesting throughout the streets of the Arab world. Calls for an "Obama Doctrine" in the region have become louder, urging clarity behind the United States' regional strategy and goals. However, it is not that US policy has been misguided; rather, it is that the White House's messaging has been sluggish and ineffective. While it has demanded that the universal right of peaceful protest be ensured in all places, it must also be clear that America's actions will be dictated by its strategic interests and priorities and those of its allies in the region.

Speaking at the US-Islamic World Forum recently, Secretary of State Hillary Clinton finally began to clarify the U.S. approach, stating that she rejected a "one-size fits all approach" to the Arab uprisings.[3] Indeed, US policy looks different in Bahrain and Syria than it does in Libya—due to the fact that US interests are very different in each arena. In her remarks, Clinton announced that President Obama would soon make a major speech on the challenges in the broader Middle East. When he does, the president will be required to answer his critics in a manner that recognizes the gap between US political ideals and the realpolitik of its strategic national interests, while judiciously considering the real interests of its allies.

In the case of Bahrain, the United States should not obfuscate: Bahrain is the central battleground of a cold war occurring today between Saudi Arabia, representing the Sunni Arab world on one side, and Iran, representing Persian and Arab Shiites on the other. America, along with the vast majority of the Sunni Arab states, has a clear and vital interest in limiting the expansion of Iranian influence, which threatens to significantly destabilize and radicalize the democratic trends sweeping the region. Meanwhile, in Yemen, the US is supporting the Gulf Cooperation Council-sponsored plan to transfer power from the long-time US-backed President Ali Abdullah Saleh to

---

3 Elise Labott, "Clinton: Changing Arab leaders not enough to bring reform," *CNN*, April 13, 2011, http://www.cnn.com/2011/POLITICS/04/13/clinton.arab.reform/index.html.

153

his Vice President, Abd Rabbuh Mansur Hadi.[4] In Yemen, our interests are equally clear: continued and enhanced cooperation with the Yemeni government to clamp down on al-Qaida, which has turned to Yemen as its preferred recruiting and training base. In both Gulf-area hot spots, the US should continue to voice support for peaceful protests and the rule of law, but we should also be clear that we have red lines, such as disallowing the growth of the extremist influence of Iran and al-Qaida.

Numerous questions have been generated from the United States' lack of a response to the growing unrest in Syria. With more than 500 protestors now killed, and anti-government protests seemingly growing each day, the Obama administration has yet to respond forcefully beyond rhetorical gestures in opposition to violence against the demonstrators, not even recalling its newly placed ambassador for consultation. Here, the United States has been reluctant because of its investment in engaging Syrian President Bashar al-Assad, in hopes that in transforming his strategic calculations, Syria could serve to usher in a new era of stability in the region, particularly in regards to Lebanon, Israel, and Iraq. Thus far, that engagement strategy has proved unsuccessful. President Assad and his regime are no longer redeemable, and with violence mounting, the US must now be prepared to work with the international community to ramp up the pressure on his regime and bring about its collapse. To suggest that chaos would ensue once the Assad regime is gone is baseless. United States senators from both political parties have urged the White House to begin supporting Syrian opposition groups,[5] and the administration should redouble its efforts in this regard. However, even more so, the White House should encourage bodies like the International Criminal Court, which this week suggested that Assad could be brought to trial for crimes against his people,[6] to take action, as well as impose greater sanctions on those Syrian officials implicated in violence, with the support of the United Nations Security Council.

While turning to the international community to build pressure on Assad would serve to advance US interests in Syria, in Libya the United States must refrain from taking a backseat to NATO in attaining our strategic interests and the interests of the Libyan people. How many more Libyan people must die before we say enough is enough?

4 David Jackson, "Obama backs transfer of power in Yemen," *USA Today*, April 24, 2011, http://content.usatoday.com/communities/theoval/post/2011/04/obama-backs-transfer-of-power-in-yemen/1#.UehJx21cXe8.
5 Michael Bowman, "US Senators Urge Non-Military Intervention in Syria," *Voice of America*, April 23, 2011, http://www.voanews.com/content/us-senators-urge-non-military-intervention-in-syria-120569589/138462.html.
6 Adrian Blomfield, "Syria: President Bashar al-Assad faces indictment by the International Criminal Court," *The Telegraph*, April 24, 2011, http://www.telegraph.co.uk/news/worldnews/middleeast/syria/8471338/Syria-President-Bashar-al-Assad-faces-indictment-by-the-International-Criminal-Court.html.

Qaddafi is finished and can no longer govern. NATO's disorganized effort indicates that the United States is required to lead; it must not shy away from this responsibility.

The recent reports that the United States has begun drone strikes in Libya[7] are a welcome sign that perhaps the United States recognizes the need for it to play a larger role in the military effort to safeguard the Libyan people from a potential massacre at the hands of Col. Muammar al-Qaddafi. However, the United States should also now begin to quickly support the rebels with substantial non-military and military aid. Recent reports that the paltry $25 million non-lethal military aid package set to be delivered to the Libyan rebels has been held up for a week, awaiting approval from the White House,[8] is shameful. As the situation in Libya risks descending into a protracted stalemate—which was inherently avoidable—regional leaders are watching President Obama to see if he has what it takes to get the job done. His response could impact the weight of US influence throughout the broader region, from Morocco to Afghanistan. President Obama's reluctance to lead another US-led military intervention in the Middle East is understandable. He was elected as the anti-Bush candidate, opposed to the war in Iraq and intent on concluding the war in Afghanistan. However, we cannot allow the trauma— or the mistakes— of previous conflicts to dictate our approach to the pressing ones that must be dealt with in earnest. The Libyan tragedy, unlike our adventure in Iraq, puts to test both our moral bent and leadership to lead.

In fact, Morocco offers an example of a country where the US can use its diplomatic ties to encourage the already burgeoning process of political reforms. Protests returned to Morocco this week, but they remain peaceful and protesters recognize that progress has been made to reform Morocco's constitution.[9] U.S. interests could be strengthened if it were to significantly support King Mohammed's efforts to demonstrate that regional leaders need not be deposed in disgrace and bloodshed, but rather can adapt their rule through gradual but real reforms and still thrive at the helm of their adapted nations.

The United States should also stand ready to support Jordan's King Abdullah. Like Mohammed in Morocco, Abdullah has demonstrated a proclivity for reform. And also like Morocco, the protests in Jordan have thus far been limited in size and scope. The United States' policy to both nations should be to support their political reformation by bolstering economic growth through projects that will ensure sustainable

---

7 Julian E. Barnes, "U.S. Launches Drone Strikes in Libya," *The Wall Street Journal*, April 22, 2011, http://online.wsj.com/article/SB10001424052748704889404576277413211029304.html.
8 Josh Rogin, "U.S. aid to Libya opposition held up at White House," *Foreign Policy*, April 21, 2011, http://thecable.foreignpolicy.com/posts/2011/04/21/us_aid_to_libyan_opposition_held_up_at_white_house.
9 Martin Jay, "Moroccan protesters reject king's draft constitution," *CNN*, April 25, 2011, http://www.cnn.com/2011/WORLD/africa/04/24/morocco.protests/index.html.

development and education. Several hundred million dollars with matching funds from oil rich Arab countries dedicated to participatory sustainable development could do wonders in countries like Jordan and Morocco. Doing so would serve to prove that partnering with the United States can lead to greater prosperity and stability.

The outcome of all of the aforementioned arenas could very well be determined by what occurs in Egypt. The Arab world is looking to its largest and most influential nation to navigate the waters of its unexpected revolution and newfound political dialogue. The Egyptian revolution has passed its first phase, but real challenges are now being faced—and they are just the beginning. At this stage, pushing for immediate and sweeping political reforms would be counter-productive. Egypt, more than any other Arab country, must be provided with the means to engage in a massive sustainable economic development program that can empower its people. The Egyptian people rightfully want freedom and food, but not freedom without food. As the Washington Post reported this week, the continued chaos in Egypt has led some Egyptians to actually support the continuation of the emergency law—the repeal of which was one of the central demands of the throngs of protestors in Tahrir Square.[10] However, the key to lifting the law, and maintaining genuine internal stability, is economic opportunity while safeguarding the Israeli-Egyptian peace treaty to ensure regional stability. This will be the test of Egypt's transition, and the United States must stand ready to do all it can to guide and help.

Unfortunately, the White House is beginning to act as though it is resigned to accepting the analysis of pundits across the globe, that US influence is on the decline and perhaps is irrecoverable. This is nonsense. Genuine leadership from the United States can and must be applied if the broader Middle East is to navigate through the Arab awakening to establish a more secure and stable region, which remains central to ending the Arab-Israeli conflict.

It is high time that President Obama realizes this, and articulates that while there is not—nor should there be—a single template for responding to the individual circumstances of each nation throughout the region experiencing unrest, the United States does have significant and specific interests at stake. In doing so, President Obama need not forfeit America's political ideals, but he must advance a strategy to safeguard the US and its allies' interests while reestablishing the United States' moral authority to lead.

---

10 "Protesters press for voice in Egyptian democracy," *USA Today*, February 13, 2011, http://usatoday30.usatoday.com/news/world/2011-02-12-egypt-revolution_N.htm.

THE ARAB SPRING

POLITICAL REFORMS MUST BE ACCOMPANIED BY ECONOMIC DEVELOPMENTS

NOVEMBER 1, 2011

Whereas political reforms are needed and necessary, no Arab country is ready for comprehensive rapid democratic reforms without an orderly and purposeful transitional period accompanied (if not preceded) by concurrent economic development programs. Indeed, instead of producing the desired outcome of a free and vibrant new social and political order, rapid political reforms without an economic development program could usher in a period of continued instability. Potentially, this would pave the way for the re-emergence of totalitarian regimes who will assume power under the pretext of maintaining order and stability.

Opposition political parties in Egypt, Tunisia, and now Libya were not given enough time and a real opportunity to organize or campaign freely in an effective way. There is no culture of political development and limited experience in country-wide political campaigns, stifling the growth of civic participation. For this reason, a minimum transitional period of two years will be needed to allow for the development of secular political parties, not only to establish their political agendas, but to be in a position to promulgate their political platforms in a free atmosphere.

For all intents and purposes, the only political party that can quickly surface as a major political force in Egypt, for example, is the Muslim Brotherhood, which has quietly but effectively been organizing for many years. If a truly free and fair election is to be held in November 2011 as planned, the Brotherhood will emerge as a powerful political party with the ability to influence government policies whether it becomes part of the ruling government or remains in the opposition. The electoral victory of the Islamist party, Ennahda, in the first elections in post-Ben-Ali Tunisia in October (only ten months after ousting the old regime) is an indication of what would happen in Egypt.

The same can be said about Libya. The planned general elections should be postponed at least two years. Indeed, elections in the near term, as the US and EU countries are prone to push for, would be a catastrophic mistake for Libya, which Qaddafi has deliberately left in shambles. Political parties must be given time and resources to organize, develop political platforms, and familiarize the public with their stance on various issues affecting the country's future security and economic developments. Opting for elections too soon would give much credence and undue power to isolated tribal factions and

157

Islamists, especially the Libyan Islamic Fighting Group (LIFG), which is the only likely group to be able to garner loyalty in the immature Libyan political landscape.

That said, Islam, both as a religion and culture, is and will always remain an integral part of any new emerging political order. In fact, Islamic parties could be a natural ally of economic development, since the majority of their activities have historically been in providing social services at the grassroots level. The main concern here is that the Arab youth are wary about allowing the boundaries of politics and religion to blur. They do not want to substitute current ruthless leaders with what Islamist rule has brought to Iran—oppression, deprivation, and disdain.

The dangers inherent in quick political reforms do not stop, however, at the advent of Islamic parties to power. Any government that would follow a truncated timeframe for elections will most likely lack the required legitimacy to rule and broad public support, especially under a revolutionary upheaval. In an immature political culture, the challenges to this sort of government would range from endless legal disputes in administrative and constitutional courts (if they exist at all) to organized violence by groups who feel they were unjustifiably unrepresented. Second, and more importantly, this kind of government cannot possibly expect to deliver the public's requirements of advances in salaries, services, and economic development which are in and of themselves the major cause of uprising.

Therefore, an essential part of the transition period in each Arab country is a new economic development program driven by the participatory planning approach to help immediately meet critical human needs and introduce and instill democratic practices at the local level—which, if done effectively, will inform how the political parties and their members operate. In the Egyptian case, and in many other Arab states, it is important to have this transitional period from authoritarian rule to democracy and a more inclusive market economy to enable a peaceful process to unfold.

Therefore, critical to peaceful and orderly transition is the immediate undertaking of economic development projects that must begin now to provide economic relief to the multitude of Arab youth who are despondent and in need of basic commodities. In fact, it was deprivation and economic inequality even more than political freedom that led to the uprising, and that is why revolutionaries and laborers in Egypt alike continued with demonstrations and strikes, because the fall of the regime did not bring what they need – food, jobs, health care, and education.

An essential cause of the Arab uprising is economic underdevelopment. Governments tended to favor state-run development projects and cut off economies from international trade and finance. It is no wonder that unemployment rates in these countries have always been in the double-digits.[11] When these countries recently moved from the socialist economic model to engage in liberalization and privatization of their economies, the liberalization process did not lead to the creation of sustainable development programs that could serve as the new source of legitimacy for the regime or enhance its stability. Instead, partly because of state corruption and partly because of mismanagement, they only lead to exacerbating socioeconomic inequality while creating a new class of super wealthy entrepreneurs – many of them affiliated with the leaders' families – who themselves become the target of public discontent.

Morocco in its post-protest approach is trying to wed democracy and development together so that each is advanced by way of the other, which serves as a good start (perhaps even a model) for reform. Sustainable development is to occur through democratic exchanges and consensus-building, and democracy is to be built during the process of creating sustainable development. Decentralization, which transfers managerial authority, skills, and capacities to sub-national levels, is Morocco's chosen framework to synergistically advance democracy and development from the bottom-up.

Considering Morocco's stated goal of decentralization, it follows that its organizational arrangement emphasizes the "participatory method." This democratic approach is to be applied by local communities together, assessing their development challenges and opportunities and creating and implementing action plans that reflect their shared priorities, such as job creation, education, health, and the environment. By extension, the monarchy is apparently open to transformative change in the whole of society, but through a bottom-up process driven by developmentally empowered and self-reliant local communities. These communities are integrated in a decentralized national system and whose elected leaders are chosen based on their ability to help forge and respond to the consensus decisions of their constituents.

An integral part of the sustainable development model is the existing Non-Government Organizations (NGOs), which should be invited to take part in it. Generally, NGOs have a great commitment toward democratic processes and enlisting people's ideas and material contributions for development interventions. Due to the urgency for development projects in countries such as Egypt, Libya, Tunisia, and others, and given the governments' ability to provide flexibility to respond to the particular socio-economic circumstances of their ever-increasing populations, the participatory sustainable development approach is not only immediately needed but

---

11 According to the CIA World Factbook, Libya's 2004 estimated unemployment rate is 30%, Tunisia's stands at 17.4%, and Egypt's, while the lowest, remains at 13.5% (the latter at 2012 estimates). For further information, see "Country Comparison: Unemployment Rate," CIA World Factbook, accessed July 19, 2013, https://www.cia.gov/library/publications/the-world-factbook/rankorder/2129rank.html?countryname=Egypt&countrycode=eg&regionCode=afr&rank=134#eg.

becomes central to sustainable political reforms. What adds tremendous credence to this approach is the fact that participatory development projects are economically feasible, especially in poorer countries, as they generally entail limited capital, require less advanced technologies and can be done on a large scale.

To be sure, there is an inherent relationship between political and economic reforms. In developing and underdeveloped countries in particular, the relationship is ever more intertwined; thus, for either to succeed, it is essential to move on both tracks simultaneously.

THE ARAB SPRING: A NEW ERA IN A TRANSFORMING GLOBE

NOVEMBER 8, 2011

The Arab uprising must be seen as an integral part of a world in transformation. The technological and informational revolutions that have spurred (and continue to spur) globalization and interconnectedness between cultures make it impossible for tyrants to rule for the entirety of their lifetimes while mercilessly subjugating their peoples to lives of servitude with no prospect of ever tasting the true meaning of freedom.

There are many who suggest, including the notable scholar George Friedman, that the Arab Spring is some kind of mass delusion that amounts to, "just some demonstrations accompanied by slaughter and extraordinarily vacuous observers."[12] When university graduate-turned-street vendor Mohamed Bouazizi set himself on fire in front of a government building in Sid Bouzid, Tunisia, he unleashed a torrent of long-repressed political expression in the Middle East. Through his brave self-immolation, he sent a clear message to his generation: die with dignity rather than continue to suffer the daily indignities that amount to an inconsequential life. It is that message that empowered Egyptians, Yemenis, Libyans, Syrians, and others to protest and die in the hope that their sacrifices would bring an end to their daily injustices and disdain.

To be sure, the ethos of protest began growing in the Arab world several years ago. In their 2007 *National Interest* article entitled "Arab Spring Fever," Nathan J. Brown and Amr Hamzawy aptly observed that the unusual protests in the streets of the Middle East from 2005-2007 only indicated that "dreams of democratic openings, competitive elections, the rule of law and wider political freedoms have captured the imagination of clear majorities in the Arab world."[13]

This new generation of Arab youth is not the same youth of a generation ago as they have been exposed to the world at large, have risen against oppression, deprivation and stagnation, and no longer wish to live in submission to corrupt leaders and governments. To assume that the Arab youth will indefinitely remain subjugated to the whims of despots is nothing short of being oblivious to the advent of a new era of Arab countries in the midst of a global transformation that cannot (and will not) exclude the Arab youth from yearning for a meaningful life. No Arab government, however

---

12 George Friedman, "Obama and the Arab Spring," *Geopolitical Weekly*, May 24, 2011, http://www.stratfor.com/weekly/20110523-obama-and-arab-spring.

13 Amr Hamzawy and Nathan J. Brown, "Arab Spring Fever," *The National Interest Online*, August 29, 2007, http://m.ceip.org/2007/08/29/arab-spring-fever/8ikc&lang=en.

oppressive, will ever be in a position to completely shut down their youths' access to the outside world and stifle their hunger for freedom.

The 2011 uprisings were neither instigated by outside powers or criminal gangs (as some Arab leaders have alluded) nor did the revolutionaries need to blame outside entities for their problems. The Arab youth refused to ask for foreign intervention unless faced with regimes willing to commit massacres to maintain power, such as Qaddafi's Libya or presently, Assad's Syria. Nor did the youth blame Israel or the United States for their country's failures; rather, their attention was turned to the failure of their own leaders and their own dictatorial governments.

The regimes of Mubarak, Assad, Qaddafi, and Saleh have typically attempted to portray the uprising as a foreign-instigated conspiracy. This has been done in vain, as the revolting youth refuse to be distracted by old, empty slogans and contrived excuses of those in power that suggest that chaos will dominate in their absence should they be ousted from power. Gone are the days when Arab leaders could ride the wave of public discontent by blaming Israel, the United States, or former colonial powers for their trying existence.

The uprisings of past and present have been organized via online social networking sites such as Facebook and Twitter, and then these massages were televised, texted, and tweeted. *Al-Jazeera*, which gained popularity and credibility among the Arab populace throughout the previous decade, has marginalized state media coverage through its accessibility and perceived impartiality, and delivered messages to ordinary, less-connected masses. Obviously, these networking and media technology tools did not make political revolutions happen. Rather, they have been on the frontline of the revolutions, precluding the need for ideological leadership to direct the revolutions. Attempts by the regimes to cut off their populations from the rest of the world by shutting down telephone and internet services proved counterproductive as it only made blatant the fact that rulers were attempting to cover up their people's outrage and widely confirmed the regime's lack of responsibility towards its own people.

New media has enabled revolutions to spread domestically, as well as beyond national borders. Arab regimes have demonstrated an outstanding success in offsetting Iran's attempt to export its Islamic revolution, but failed miserably to oppress the Arab Spring because, as F. Gregory Gause has argued, this, "very leaderless quality of the popular mobilizations...seems to have made them sources of inspiration."[14] But it has also rendered the mobilization impervious to the security apparatus. That is why the protest that started over rampant unemployment and corruption in Tunisia, and the ousting of Tunisian

14 F. Gregory Gause, "Why Middle East Studies Missed the Arab Spring: The Myth of Authoritarian Stability," *Foreign Affairs* 90, Issue 4 (2011): 87.

President Zine El Abidine Ben Ali, has led to protests throughout the Arab world—from Algeria to Yemen—with a united refrain to send their respective leaders to join Ben Ali in his forced exile in Saudi Arabia. The subsequent revolt which has gripped Egypt has echoed throughout the Middle East, from Libya to Syria to Bahrain.

Contrary to what some commentators have said, the Arab uprisings are *not* a divorced phenomenon from the protests that have taken over many parts of the Western world due to the continuing economic crisis. Despite the unique characteristics of each country's situation, the common theme of the protests in the Arab world (as well as in the West) has been largely shaped by the continuing world economic crisis, expanding economic inequality, and rising social injustices. Massive budget cuts and raised taxes have led to violent protests in Britain, Spain, Italy, Greece, and elsewhere in Europe.[15]

The "Occupy Wall Street" movement sees the root cause of the social and economic inequality in corporate greed with ties to government officials and therefore targets its ire at financial institutions whose power and influence has caused the current crisis. Arabs, Europeans, Israelis, and Americans have all pointed their fingers at those they believe to be responsible for their problems.

European and American protests require a change in policies, not government. For the protesters, democracy and entrepreneurship have been exploited at the expense of the average person and they are not working well. That is why the protesters are seeking reforms and even more drastic measures including the overhauling of the entire system. Conversely, the Arab youth, who similarly claim that they are representing the "99 percent," saw the root cause of their socioeconomic misery, lack of freedom, and injustices to be the authoritarian governments that created and sustained the conditions for their misery. They have not experienced freedom and democracy and they see no prospect of effecting any meaningful change by current regimes and that is why they are seeking an "overthrow" of the system.

Regardless of how youth uprisings fluctuate in intensity, they are not a passing phenomenon. They will last for many years and will wind down only when new or current Arab regimes commit to, and deliver on, promises for constructive socio-economic and political reforms, regardless of how long that might take.

---

15 Alessandra Rizzo and Meera Selva, "Occupy Wall Street Protests Spread To Europe, Asia," *Huffington Post*, October 15, 2011, http://www.huffingtonpost.com/2011/10/15/occupy-wall-street-protests-europe-asia_n_1012336.html.

ALON BEN-MEIR

THE ARAB SPRING COULD TURN INTO
A LONG AND CRUEL WINTER

DECEMBER 12, 2011

Due to a host of common denominators in the Arab world, including the lack of traditional liberalism, tribal power, the elites' control of business, the monopoly on power by ethnic minorities, the militaries that cling to power, and the religious divide and Islamic extremism, the Arab Spring could sadly turn into a long and cruel winter. These factors are making the transformation into a more reformist governance slow, filled with hurdles, and punctuated with intense bloodshed. At the same time, each Arab country differs characteristically from one another on other dimensions, including history and culture, demographic composition, the role of the military, resources, and geostrategic situations. This combination of commonality and uniqueness has had, and will continue to have, significant impacts on how the uprising in each Arab country evolves and what kind of political order might eventually emerge.

To illustrate how complex this transformational period is, a brief review of the Arab countries that have made (or are in the midst of) revolutionary change is in order. In Bahrain, the subdued protest in the country following the Saudi intervention is misleading. The fundamental problem is that the Sunni royal family, which has been in power for more than 200 years, is not willing to relinquish any of its powers to the predominantly Shiite Muslim population through significant constitutional reforms. This has been further aggravated by the fact that the royal family sees Iran's hand in the disturbances and is terrified by the prospect of increased Iranian meddling in its internal affairs.[16] What happens in Bahrain is also of great concern to the rest of the Gulf States, especially Saudi Arabia, which explains its direct interference in Bahrain to quell the uprising with American nodding (Bahrain is the home of the US Fifth Fleet). Though the commission of an inquiry report (which has recently come out) condemned the brutal treatment of the protesters,[17] the official response was generally muted and only nominal changes were leveled against some in the security apparatus – all of which is likely to feed greater resentment toward the state which Iran is likely to encourage. The cycle of unrest interspersed with violence is prone to continue until both sides agree on

---

16 "Bahrain hints at Iranian role over country's Shia uprising," *The Guardian*, March 21, 2011, http://www.guardian.co.uk/world/2011/mar/21/bahrain-iran-role-uprising-shia.

17 Ian Black, "Bahrain inquiry accuses security forces of brutality and torture," *The Guardian*, November 23, 2011, http://www.guardian.co.uk/world/2011/nov/23/bahrain-inquiry-blames-security-forces.

a new political formula that must be acceptable to the rest of the Gulf States, as that would directly and indirectly impact their political system.

In Syria, where another religious minority – the Alawites – rules over the Sunni majority, the prospect of sectarian violence is looming large on the horizon. The mass killing of civilians by government forces and members of the Alawite community led to a significant military defection and they are now fighting back under the banner of the Free Syrian Army. Moreover, by rejecting the Arab League's (AL) initiative to end the violence, President Assad has probably lost the last opportunity for a peaceful exit, causing both the AL and Turkey to boycott his regime politically and economically. Uncontained, such a situation could probably turn into another post-Saddam Iraq, where vendettas have prevailed between the Sunnis and Shiites, especially at a time when Syria has become the battleground between Iran and Turkey, who are determined to shape the outcome of the upheaval in Syria to safeguard their national security interests and regional ambitions.

Even in those countries where the Arab Spring has already toppled the regime, the real challenges for a new political order have begun. In Tunisia, the victory by the Islamist party, Ennahda, in the parliamentary elections of October 2011 raises questions about whether or not the Islamists will remain true to the secular foundation of Tunisia. Conflict between the religious and secular forces could well turn into violence. The Islamists have already started flexing their muscles, from an attack on a secular TV channel in the capital, Tunis, by Salafi groups protesting against the broadcasted content, to the occupation of a university campus by another Islamic group demanding segregation of the sexes in class and the right for female students to wear *neqab*, a full-face veil.[18] The secular forces have staged counter-protests outside the interim parliament over how big a role Islam should play in society. It remains to be seen, however, if Tunisia's general Western orientation and fear of a counter-revolutionary movement inhibits the ruling party, Ennahda, from compromising its commitment to maintain a democratic form of government.

Egypt is faced with the dual challenge of chaos and sectarian and ideological divisions. Many Egyptians would agree that their country is already in a state of chaos with the collapse of the police force, the unprecedented rise in the crime rate, the endless strikes by professionals, the continuing conflict between Muslims and Copts and the still uncertain "road map" for a transition of power from the military to a civilian government. The current turmoil is the product of two ongoing parallel conflicts, one between Islamist and liberal forces over the nature of the future civilian government, and another between both of them and the military

18 "Tunisian secular, Islamist students clash on campus," *Al Arabiya News*, November 29, 2011, http://www.alarabiya.net/articles/2011/11/29/179960.html.

council over the status of the army in post-Mubarak Egypt. The fact that the Islamic forces, the Muslim Brotherhood, and the ultraconservative Salafists have secured almost a two-thirds majority in the new parliament sends alarming signs that the Islamic forces could win in both conflicts, turning Egypt either into an Iran-like theocracy or, if a friction emerges, into a Pakistan-like failed state. The saving grace here is that the Muslim Brotherhood and the Salafists do not see eye-to-eye and the Brotherhood, thinking in the long-term, will end up making a deal with the military and form a government with some of the secular parties to keep the young, secular Egyptian happy. This cozy arrangement, however, will endure only as long as the Brotherhood keeps its commitment to constitutional democracy and the prerogatives that the military can exercise to safeguard the democratic nature of the state and its national security.

In Libya, Qaddafi's rule has come to an end, but the impact of his legacy of starving the people of any semblance of participatory governance will remain in Libya for years to come, with a high probability that it will turn into chaos or a civil war. The National Transitional Council is struggling to navigate power relations between tribes and militias, especially the Libyan Islamic Fighting Group (LIFG), whose members are veterans of the Afghan war and fought alongside al Qaeda and the Taliban.[19] LIFG seems to be the only likely group to be able to garner loyalty in the immature Libyan political landscape. Though defeated, the pro-Qaddafi supporters might not give up the fight, and they may well attempt to destabilize the political process using violence and terror, especially when policing and intelligence-capacity remains too sourly inadequate to safeguard what is left of the state establishment.

Thus, because of the different makeup of their societies there is no political panacea that the Arab states can espouse. There are, however, certain measures that can be adopted by most Arab states with some individualized adjustments to substantially shorten the revolutionary process and reduce the level of friction and violence.

First, the collective actions by the AL – along the lines of its latest punitive measures against Syria – should be taken against any Arab government that denies its population's demands for reform and resorts to violence to suppress it. This is an unprecedented and welcomed step that augurs well for the Arab states, especially if such consensus becomes institutionalized, which would give the League real power instead of being a mere debating society. By taking such measures against Syria in particular, a country that sees itself as the beating-heart of Arab nationalism, the AL sanctions have become even more significant. For the AL to maintain its credibility and enforcement abilities it must ensure that

---

19 Ian Black, "The Libyan Islamic Fighting Group – from al-Qaida to the Arab spring," *The Guardian*, September 5, 2011, http://www.guardian.co.uk/world/2011/sep/05/libyan-islamic-fighting-group-leaders.

its sanctions against Syria are genuine and are fully executed, and that other Arab states must be expected to deal with their own uprising in a manner consistent with their own collective demands from Syria. Egypt and Saudi Arabia, in particular, can play a key role in keeping the Arab League cohesive, strong, and resolute.

Second, since the Islamic parties (who have shown significant gains in Tunisia, Morocco, and now in Egypt) are slated to play leading roles in future Arab governments, to avoid counter-revolution movements they must remain true to the democratic process that brought them to power. They must remember that the Arab youth have long since rejected Iranian-style theocracy and many have died and will continue to die for freedom. That said, democratically based governments and Islam are not contradictory as long as a healthy balance between the two is created. The Turkish model, however imperfect, offers a good start and may be emulated successfully as long as checks and balances continue to govern the political process. Initial signs to this direction have appeared in the three countries, as statements were made by the winning Islamic parties – Egypt's Freedom and Justice, Tunisia's Ennahda, and Morocco's Justice and Development – that they would seek coalitions with the liberal parties, and not with the ultraconservative Salafists.[20] The West has a clear interest in encouraging this approach and allowing it the opportunity to mature into a coherent policy.

Third, it is necessary to create a transitional government for at least two years composed of non-ideologue professionals to handle all domestic issues, particularly economic development, education, healthcare, and infrastructure, and to prepare for a new constitution. Drafting a new constitution is already on the agenda of each governing body, elected or not, in the Arab Spring countries which offers a momentous opportunity to push for lasting reforms, providing religious and ethnic minorities their civil rights, while fully committing said minorities to the nation's unity and laws, even when those are within an Islamic framework. What is important to point out is that, to avoid a "dictatorship of the parliamentary majority," drafting the constitution should be done by a broader national assembly that is representative of each country's population and its political, ethnic, tribal, and religious mosaic. Drafting constitutions should also correspond to each country's specific characteristics of Islamic and liberal forces. In Egypt, for instance, the military may have to end up with a special status in the new constitution, given the army's role in the success of the revolution

---

20 David D. Kirkpatrick, "In Egypt, No Alliance With Ultraconservatives, Islamist Party Says," *The New York Times*, December 1, 2011, http://www.nytimes.com/2011/12/02/world/middleeast/egypts-muslim-brotherhood-keeps-distance-from-salafis.html; see also, "Coalition talks with Tunisia's Islamists have begun, leftist leader says," *Al Arabiya News*, October 25, 2011, http://www.alarabiya.net/articles/2011/10/25/173679.html; and, Paul Schemm, "Morocco Elections: Islamist Party Wins," *Huffington Post*, November 27, 2011, http://www.huffingtonpost.com/2011/11/27/morocco-elections-islamist-party_n_1115425.html.

but more importantly, in order to maintain the country's cohesiveness, its international commitments, and its national security.

Fourth, Arab states that have not as yet been affected by protest for change, particularly Jordan, Morocco, and the Gulf monarchies, will be wise to begin systematic socio-political and economic reforms. The constitutional amendments that King Mohammed VI of Morocco has proposed and approved in a referendum, allowing greater authority to the elected parliament but still within the monarchy,[21] offers a good start and could serve as an example for other Arab monarchies. The idea here is to direct the pace of change in a way that allows gradual democratization and avoids friction and violence that might emerge out of a sudden, uncontrolled change as happened elsewhere in the Arab world. Every Arab King or Emir can gradually relinquish some of his power to a constructional monarchy where the king or the Emir remains not only the head of the state with the trappings of their positions but remains the Commander-in-Chief of the armed forces and has the final say on all major foreign policy issues. The Prime Minister, on the other hand, is the head of the government with political powers which focus on domestic issues mandated by a popularly-elected parliament. By following this path, current Arab Kings and Emirs can still maintain their hold on power while simultaneously meeting the people's demands, which will ease the transition of their countries through the inevitable change that must occur either through violent upheaval or peaceful transition.

The Arab youth have risen and no Arab government or leader can prevent the wave of awakening that will continue to sweep the Arab world. Regardless of the kind of government many Arab states may end up with, an adherence to human rights, gradual political reforms that ensure basic freedoms, and a focus on economic development will be central to a more peaceful transition. Otherwise, the Arab Spring could sadly turn into a long and cruel winter.

---

21 "Morocco reforms to cut monarch's power," *Al Jazeera*, June 17, 2011, http://www.aljazeera.com/news/africa/2011/06/2011617172114510513.html.

PREMATURE ELECTIONS INVITE POLITICAL INSTABILITY

JULY 9, 2012

Although elections and political reforms are needed in the wake of the Arab Spring, premature elections could usher in a period of continued political instability punctuated by violence, or introduce new totalitarian regimes that would assume power under the pretext of maintaining order and stability. Of paramount importance is the forming of transitional governments proportionally representative of all segments of the population for a minimum of five years. Such a government would be tasked with writing a new constitution and instituting gradual political reforms while promoting human rights and economic development programs. Otherwise, elections will fail to produce the desired outcome of a free and vibrant new political and social order.

Indeed, no Arab country is ready for comprehensive political reforms without first developing a democratic culture, creating the environment that encourages the formation of political parties, and develops a clear political platform that is freely promoted to the public. Here, Egypt, Libya, Yemen, Iraq, and even Tunisia offer good examples of where internal socio-economic and political conditions highlight the difficulties involved. To that end, the situation in these Arab states strongly suggests that unless the following seven impediments are fully addressed, the Arab Spring will turn out to be the cruelest winter, shattering all hopes promised by the uprisings.

1. THE RUSH FOR PARLIAMENTARY ELECTIONS

The rush to hold elections invariably favors the existing social and/or political groups that are the most organized, disciplined, and rooted in society. In Egypt and Tunisia, the Islamist Muslim Brotherhood (MB) dominated the political scene. In Libya, however, although there was a strong possibility that the Libyan Islamic Fighting Group (LIFG) would win, the Islamic wave was broken and continued political instability will dominate the immature Libyan political landscape. Generally, the inability of secular and independent parties and those who share similar political orientations to coalesce around a single platform has generally boosted the performance of the Islamists, as the former had neither the time nor the means to organize politically and offer alternate political platform to the Islamists.

2. PROLIFERATION OF PARTIES

Fragmented democratic systems that use proportional representation, which translates votes to legislative power, typically see a notable proliferation of political parties that leads to the inevitable breakup of the electorate. As a consequence of the sweeping transformative effects of the Arab Spring, countries such as Egypt, Libya, and Tunisia have been pushed both internally and externally to hold premature elections, regardless of the prevailing political environments that existed prior to the revolutions. As a result, dozens of political parties were abruptly formed (81 parties contested Tunisia's elections,22 more than 40 were active in Egypt's parliamentary elections,23 and Libya, having just participated in its first and most-recent elections, has an exorbitant 130).24 This mushrooming of political parties not only confuses the public but also prevents national consensus on any major foreign or domestic issues or programs.

3. INABILITY TO ESTABLISH POLITICAL COHESIVENESS

When haste dictates the scale and scope of political campaigns, it is simply not possible for detailed platforms to be developed in time to deal with the litany of social ills that affect most, if not the entire, Middle East region. On top of the numerous political parties that are filling nascent political vacuums formed by the Arab Spring, thousands of independent candidates have thrown their hats in the electoral ring. The outbreak of independent candidates has deepened the level of political fragmentation and enhanced the bewildering nature of post-dictatorship Middle Eastern societies. The rush to elections, for example, has given Libyan candidates less than three weeks to formulate their political platforms, which makes them extremely difficult for the public to fully judge or comprehend. Consequently, candidates will hardly represent any sort of constituency in a manner that will fulfill the political aspirations of the young and the more secular parts of the electorate.

4. NO CULTURE FOR DEMOCRACY AND REFORM

Regardless of the timing of elections, talk of democratic aspirations is wholly premature in societies that have never experienced a culture of democracy and reform. From their establishment in the wake of World War I and II in the early 20th century, all Arab states were led by authoritarian regimes that have inhibited democratic expression and stunted economic development for the majority of their populations. The stunning speed and scale of the Arab Spring has thrown a wrench into the old order, but it should not follow that political reforms can or must be established in the same speed. Being that many of these countries have never had any experience with true democracy, holding immediate elections has already harmed the democratic process and set back the aspirations of those who wished to play a role in their country's political renewal.

---

22 "Background: Tunisian Elections," *Al Jazeera*, October 27, 2011, http://www.aljazeera.com/indepth/spotlight/2011/10/20111089246280661.html.

23 "Egypt holds second round of parliamentary election," *BBC News*, December 14, 2011, http://www.bbc.co.uk/news/world-middle-east-16172151.

24 Ian Black, "Libya: unpromising soil for the hopes of the Arab spring," *The Guardian*, July 9, 2012, http://www.guardian.co.uk/world/2012/jul/09/libya-parliamentary-elections-arab-spring.

5. ROLE OF THE MILITARY

In countries that have an entrenched security apparatus (the "deep state" as it is known in Egypt),[25] the results of elections will be meaningless unless efforts are made to subordinate to civilian authority several critical government agencies including the military, intelligence services, interior ministries, and secret police. Regardless of election results, the military in countries such as Egypt (and perhaps soon in Syria) will retain crucial control over the new political system in order to prevent relinquishing their inordinate power. The paramount concern for military figures is maintaining final say on national security and major foreign policy issues, and in Egypt's case, to safeguard its economic empire.

6. CONTINUED VIOLENT RESISTANCE

Many of the various parties and actors that have emerged in the burgeoning Middle Eastern democracies continue to resort to militant resistance in the face of intransigence on the part of central authorities, military or otherwise. Tahrir Square continues to be filled with friends and foes alike of the MB, in addition to the ruling military authorities.[26] In spite of the recent elections, armed militias continue to run rampant in Libya, exercising control over many parts of the national territory.[27] Syria is facing the opposite scenario as the central authority continues to employ brutal means to retain power. Since the removal of Assad has become central to the emergence of a new political order, the carnage in Syria can be expected to spread even further as the regime fights for its life.

7. LACK OF CONSENSUS AROUND THE NATURE OF REFORM

In holding elections immediately after a social revolution, there seems to be no consensus about a new constitution and the democratic reforms that should be enacted. This has turned the electoral processes in Egypt, Tunisia, and Libya into horse races of national councils, transitional authorities, and military commanders. The various types of democratic rule that can be implemented should reject quick elections, as the diverse sectarian societies found in the Middle East need to be reconciled with elementary premises of political and human freedoms. Indeed, the tribal nature of Libya, for example, had engendered a debate between adopting federalism over decentralization, the latter clearly favoring tribal communities

---

25 Matthew Kaminski, "The Return of Egypt's 'deep state,'" *The Wall Street Journal*, June 15, 2012, http://online.wsj.com/article/SB10001424052702303734204577468642662667770.html.

26 "'No to the Brotherhood' protest expected in Egypt's Tahrir Square," *Al Arabiya*, July 6, 2012, http://english.alarabiya.net/articles/2012/07/06/224795.html.

27 Alex Spillius, "Libyan armed militias 'have stranglehold on country,'" *The Telegraph*, July 5, 2012, http://www.telegraph.co.uk/news/worldnews/africaandindianocean/libya/9376982/Libyan-armed-militias-have-stranglehold-on-country.html.

and a preferred option in Libya as a federalist system could exacerbate tense pre-existing ethnic and tribal conflicts.[28]

Regardless of how well-handled these reforms are and however long they may take, political reforms in and of themselves are insufficient unless accompanied by sustainable economic development programs. The public does not want just freedom—they want food, jobs, health care, education, and a promising future. Genuine democratic reforms will take decades to evolve. Sooner or later, no Arab state will escape meaningful political change. The rush to elections, however, does not support permanent change and makes a mockery of the democratic ideals that so many have died for.

28 "Libyan Elections Likely To Hinge on Tribal Ties," *Al-Monitor*, July 5, 2012, http://www.al-monitor.com/pulse/politics/2012/07/libyans-heading-toward-constitue.html.

SUSTAINABLE ECONOMIC DEVELOPMENT: CENTRAL TO THE DURABILITY OF POLITICAL REFORMS IN ARAB STATES

JULY 16, 2012

There is a pressing need in the Arab states, especially the countries with nascent democratic restructuring such as Egypt, Tunisia, and Libya, to adopt sustainable development projects in parallel to, and concurrent with, political reforms in order for the latter to endure and develop further. Indeed, these countries that faced popular uprisings and rushed to hold elections will continue to experience political instability not only because they have never developed a culture of democracy but also because the public wants more than the right to vote. These newly-formed governments must find the means, especially through sustainable development projects, to provide the public with their basic needs, or they will soon face another upheaval, no matter how committed these governments remain to political reforms.

The root causes of the many regional uprisings stem primarily from the deprivation and economic inequalities suffered by the majority of Middle East populations. Historically, Arab governments tended to favor state-run development projects and exercise near-to-complete control of their economies,[29] which exacerbated socioeconomic inequalities and created a new class of enriched elites, many of whom benefitted from the largesse of autocratic regimes (Syria and Libya being good examples of this). When these countries moved from the socialist economic model to engagement in the liberalization and privatization of their economies, the neoliberal processes did not lead to sustainable and egalitarian development that could serve as a new source of legitimacy for the regime or enhance its stability.

Though the overturning of despotic regimes in Tunisia, Libya, and Egypt can be counted as tangible successes, the reality is that vast numbers of youth in these countries (and throughout the Middle East) remain despondent. They want food, health care, education, and the opportunity to grow and prosper with dignity. If peaceful and orderly transitions are to be the reality, there must be an immediate concurrent undertaking of sustainable economic development projects. Such projects may include the farming of produce and animals including poultry, planting fruit trees, building irrigation systems, reclaiming wasteland, and scores of other projects. The great benefit in engaging in sustainable development is that small communities are empowered to collectively decide on projects of their choice from which they can benefit, while

---

29 Gudrun Kramer, "Liberalization and Democratization in the Arab World," *Middle East Report* 22 (January/ February 1992): http://www.merip.org/mer/mer174/liberalization-democratization-arab-world.

the principles of democratic culture are simultaneously fostered through the need for majority consensus about any project that the community decides to adopt. Moreover, such projects require limited capital and employ less-sophisticated technologies without the need for a continuous infusion of money or new technologies before these projects develop a strong financial base.[30]

Sustainable economic development invariably creates wealth both for the communities that adopt such projects and for the state treasury, which can generate more income through increased tax revenues and in turn can be used toward improving the social safety net and the overall health of the economy.[31] Moreover, given that these projects are community-orientated and designed to create local wealth, providing block loans or financial assistance directly to the state, however large, will not serve a broader (or moral) societal purpose. In giving money directly to communities, however, governmental agencies such as the United States Agency for International Development (USAID) could go a long way in financing thousands of community projects from the bottom-up. Such an approach makes it possible to locally enhance education, achieve better health care, and develop the necessary infrastructure that allows for the expansion and sale of the product that the community has created.

In addition to international organizations, domestic non-governmental organizations (NGOs) can play an integral part in ensuring the success of the sustainable development model. Due to the participatory principles that formed them, NGOs have a greater commitment toward democratic processes while enlisting people's ideas and material contributions for developmental interventions without threatening the government. The goals of local communities organized by NGOs reflect local interests more than government-driven initiatives. The resources NGOs procure locally or through international donors to help marshal development include a mix of educational, technical, and material support. The United States, for instance, could dramatically expand the Peace Corps from its current total of around 10,000[32] to well over 100,000 and increase its financial aid, which proportionately pales in comparison to France or the United Kingdom.[33]

When communities choose their own projects based on their immediate needs through collective decision-making (based on advice and consent), the basis of democracy is developed. Morocco's post-protest approach, for example, to "wed [democracy

30 Yossef Ben-Meir, "Morocco: Democracy-Building and Sustainable Development," *Morocco Board*, March 13, 2011, http://www.moroccoboard.com/news/34-news-release/5145-morocco-democracy-building-and-sustainable-development.

31 Ibid.

32 "Fast Facts," *Peace Corps*, updated July 16, 2012, http://www.peacecorps.gov/about/fastfacts/.

33 Talea Miller and Larisa Epatko, "Foreign Aid Facing Proposed Cuts and a Public Perception Problem," *PBS NewsHour*, March 10, 2011, http://www.pbs.org/newshour/rundown/2011/03/foreign-aid-facing-proposed-cuts-public-perception-problem.html.

and development] together so that each is advanced by way of the other,"[34] can serve as a good model for reform (albeit still on a small scale). Morocco's stated goal of decentralization emphasizes the "participatory method," a democratic approach applied by local communities to assess their development challenges and opportunities, and create and implement action plans that reflect their shared priorities.

Apart from Morocco, Israel has had notable success in the area of sustainable development. The Kibbutz[35] and Moshav[36] movements, for instance, sought to base their development on collectivity and self-reliance. Before the formation of the State of Israel, the early Jewish settlers overcame poverty through community development and methods of settlement. Notwithstanding the hostilities between Israel and many of the Arab states, Israel's eminent success in sustainable development offers a model that can be emulated by most underdeveloped and developing Arab states.

In contrast to states that have experimented with sustainable development, others in the Middle East region, notably the Gulf States such as Saudi Arabia and Bahrain, had to "buy" their populations off with generous handouts in order to pacify them in an effort to quell the region's revolutionary trend from knocking down their doors.[37] By doing so, the concentration of power is left in the hands of the government, and the political status and financial dependence remain unaffected. Indeed, sustainable development could theoretically pose a threat to the existing governance, as it directly empowers people to work within their own communities and take control over issues that affect their daily lives. That said, those Arab countries that have not experienced a social uprising (the Arab Spring) as of yet can avoid being swept up by the revolutionary fervor if preference is given to sustainable development rather than resorting to "handouts" to stultify their populations, which offers only a transient respite.

The uprising in Egypt, following Libya's revolution and Tunisia's "Jasmine Revolution," opened a new chapter of change in the Arab world. For the long-entrenched Arab regimes to avoid the same fate as the regimes in Tunisia, Egypt, Libya, and Syria, they must heed the powerful message being expressed on the streets

34 Yossef Ben-Meir.
35 Jon Fidler, "Focus on Israel- Kibbutz," *Israel Ministry of Foreign Affairs*, November 1, 2002, http://www.mfa.gov.il/MFA/MFAArchive/2000_2009/2002/11/Focus%20on%20Israel-%20Kibbutz.
36 "The Moshav," *Jewish Virtual Library*, accessed July 12, 2012, http://www.jewishvirtuallibrary.org/jsource/Society_&_Culture/moshavim.html.
37 See Caryle Murphy, "Saudi Arabia's King Abudllah promises $36 billion in benefits," *Christian Science Monitor*, February 23, 2011, http://www.csmonitor.com/World/Middle-East/2011/0223/Saudi-Arabia-s-King-Abdullah-promises-36-billion-in-benefits, and "Bahrain doles out money to families," *Al Jazeera*, February 12, 2011, http://www.aljazeera.com/news/middleeast/2011/02/201121251854857192.html.

throughout the region. Some Arab tyrants, such as Assad of Syria, may *temporarily* succeed in subduing popular resistance, but it will take tremendous violence to achieve that. Realizing the inevitability of change, however, Arab governments should now rethink their approach by adopting gradual and political reforms that must be accompanied with sustainable participatory development projects including, if not especially, the countries that have already gone through the revolutionary process. In doing so, and as long as the public is clear and trusts their governments' commitment in this regard, these governments can avoid a potential new upheaval, as the Arab Spring is not a passing phenomenon. Indeed, no Arab government should engage in wishful thinking as the Arab youth have finally been awakened to a reality that they are no longer willing to accept, however long the struggle may take.

In the final analysis, the democratic dividends that can be reaped from the Arab Spring will be squandered unless accompanied by sustainable development projects. By following this path, local communities will be empowered through decentralization and consensus-building while fostering durable democratic principles with sustainable economic growth.